AVIATION TERRORISM AND SECURITY

CASS SERIES ON POLITICAL VIOLENCE

ISSN 1365-0580

Series Editors – DAVID C. RAPOPORT, University of California, Los Angeles
PAUL WILKINSON, University of St Andrews, Scotland

1. *Terror from the Extreme Right*, edited by Tore Bjørgo
2. *Millennialism and Violence*, edited by Michael Barkun
3. *Religious Radicalism in the Greater Middle East*, edited by
   Bruce Maddy-Weitzman and Efraim Inbar
4. *The Revival of Right-Wing Extremism in the Nineties*, edited by
   Peter H. Merkl and Leonard Weinberg
5. *Violence in Southern Africa*, edited by William Gutteridge and J.E. Spence

AVIATION TERRORISM AND SECURITY

Edited by

Paul Wilkinson and Brian M. Jenkins

FRANK CASS

LONDON and PORTLAND, OR

First published in 1999 in Great Britain by
FRANK CASS PUBLISHERS
Newbury House, 900 Eastern Avenue,
London, IG2 7HH

and in the United States of America by
FRANK CASS PUBLISHERS
c/o ISBS
5804 N.E. Hassalo Street
Portland, Oregon 97213-3644

Website: http://www.frankcass.com

British Library Cataloguing in Publication Data

Aviation terrorism and security. – (Cass series on
political violence; no. 6)
1. Airports – Security measures. 2. Terrorism – Prevention
3. Hijacking of aircraft – Prevention
I. Wilkinson, Paul, 1937– II. Jenkins, Brian
363.2`876

ISBN 0 7146 4906 6 (cloth)
ISBN 0 7146 4463 3 (paper)

Library of Congress Cataloguing in Publication Data

Aviation terrorism and security / edited by Paul Wilkinson and Brian Jenkins
        p.   cm. – (Cass series on political violence)
Includes bibliographical references and index.
    ISBN 0-7146-4906-6 (hardcover : alk. paper). – ISBN 0-7146-4463-3
(pbk. : alk. paper)
    1. Airports – Security measures. 2. Hijacking of aircraft.
3. Terrorism – Prevention. 4. Aeronautics, Commercial – Security
measures. I. Wilkinson, Paul, 1937–   . II. Jenkins, Brian
Michael. III. Series.
HE9797.4.S4A94   1998   98-46469
363.28′76–dc21   CIP

This group of studies first appeared in a Special Issue on 'Aviation Terrorism and
Security' in *Terrorism and Political Violence* 10/3 (Autumn 1998)
published by Frank Cass.

Printed in Great Britain by
Antony Rowe Ltd, Chippenham

Contents

1

Introduction

PAUL WILKINSON and BRIAN M. JENKINS

The aims of this volume are: first, to assess the changing terrorist threat to the security of civil aviation, including newly emerging threats; second, to review the effectiveness of some of the major policies and measures introduced at national and international levels to protect civil aviation; and third, to consider the merits of new or hitherto neglected approaches to preventing and combatting aviation terrorism.

A key advantage shared by our contributors is that in addition to their expertise in aviation terrorism and security they have a wide knowledge and understanding of the post-Cold War strategic environment and patterns of conflict. This provides the essential context for analysing not only the ever-changing phenomena of international and domestic terrorism worldwide, but also for interpreting the significant developments in aviation terrorism that are in large part shaped by these factors. If we fail to adequately understand the dynamics of the relationship between patterns of violence and conflict generally, and aviation terrorism in particular, how can we hope accurately to identify new threats and develop more effective means to counter them?

Ariel Merari's opening essay provides a fascinating statistical analysis of aviation terrorism trends since the upsurge of modern international terrorism in the late 1960s and early 1970s. Many non-specialists may be surprised at his depressing conclusion that, in spite of the significant improvements in aviation security achieved by certain countries and the efforts of international organisations such as the International Civil Aviation Organisation (ICAO):

In the recent decade, the average hijacker had an 81 per cent chance of actually seizing control of the airliner. The terrorist hijacker had an even higher chance of success – 85 per cent. The rate of success in bombing attacks against airlines, the principal cause of death in attacks on commercial aviation, has also been appallingly high – 76 per cent.

A great strength of Professor Merari's analysis is that it is both historically comprehensive and encompasses all the major forms of aviation terrorism – attacks on airlines, airports and airline offices.

Ariel Merari observes that 'even in the recent decade, the rate of attacks is still quite high'. Hence, despite the decline in the overall numbers of attacks on airliners during the 30 year period, 'the rate of attacks is still quite high. The magnitude of the threat is still a reason for worry'. Complacent assumptions that the threat from aviation terrorism faded away after Lockerbie should be discarded. In 1996, the last year of Professor Merari's analysis, just over 10 per cent of all recorded acts of international terrorism were directed at aviation targets. They included a dozen hijackings, two attempted hijackings, half a dozen attacks on airline officers and an airport bombing; the year culminated in the crash of the hijacked Ethiopian Airlines Boeing 767 off the Comoro Islands with the loss of 127 lives. We need to add to this picture events such as the conviction of Ramzi Yousef for conspiring to create what US prosecutors called '48 hours of terror in the sky' by plotting to bomb a dozen US airliners in mid-air in the Pacific region, the growing number of man-portable SAM attacks on aircraft, and the ominous possibility of terrorists emulating the Aum Shinrikyo Sarin gas attack on the Tokyo subway system, possibly by attacking a civil aviation target such as an airliner cabin or an airport lounge or terminal building.

Of course it is important to see the statistics on aviation terrorism in their proper context. In reality airlines are an extremely safe means of transport. In each decade since the mid-1940s, there has been a 40 per cent fall in the fatal accident rate for international scheduled flights. Indeed it is the incredibly good safety record of the world's airlines that has helped to make air travel such a phenomenally successful mode of transport and one of the fastest growing industries in the world.

There is a compelling case to be made for an effective security system on grounds of the commercial interests of the civil aviation industry. The second Gulf War showed that if the public develop a real fear of flying and no longer trust the will and capability of governments and aviation authorities to prevent and deter terrorist attacks, they will desert the airways in droves. In the first week of the war, The Association of European Airlines claimed that its members had lost 25 per cent of their traffic. *Airline Business* estimated that the industry as a whole was losing approximately $1.5 billion per month in the immediate aftermath of the war. The industry has every reason to be apprehensive about the effects of any future major conflict in the Middle East, and the concomitant threat of increased terrorism. What counts is the public's *perception* of the risks involved.

Yet despite the strong desire of both passengers and crew for effective security against terrorism, and despite the real improvements in aviation security made by certain states following the Lockerbie bombing, many major security weaknesses and vulnerable points remain. Moreover, as Ariel Merari reminds us, these gaps are by no means confined to the poorer countries in the developing world:

> ... in North America the rate of thwarting of hijackings over the recent two decades has been 43 per cent and in Western Europe 24 per cent (still, a better than two-to-one and three-to-one chance for the average hijacker, respectively). Yet in the most recent decade the thwarting rate in North America had dropped to 23 per cent and in Western Europe to merely eight per cent. The rate of foiling of bombing of airliners also leaves much to be desired. In North America it was 22 per cent over the most recent two decades ... and in Western Europe, 60 per cent.

Ariel Merari's explanation for this sorry situation is twofold: the security authorities have almost invariably failed to foresee the terrorist's adoption of fresh methods of attacking aviation, and there is a basic lack of expert knowledge and professionalism on the part of the airline companies' security systems.

The essays by Peter St John and Brian Jenkins provide ample evidence on the lack of foresight displayed by the security authorities when they were faced by the first wave of hijacks for political extortion and the first sabotage bombings of airliners respectively. It is true that aviation security systems did adapt quite rapidly to the threat from the wave of hijackings in the early 1970s, but they have been much slower in their response to the threat of sabotage bombing. Far too many airports still lack the enhanced x-ray machines capable of reliably detecting explosives, and many are still failing to operate an effective and comprehensive system of positive baggage reconciliation, the linchpin of good security against the sabotage bomb.

In his examination of the development of the hijacking tactic by terrorists, Peter St John concentrates on the political motivation of perpetrators of aviation terrorism as his prime causal factor of hijackings, attacks on airports and sabotage of civil aircraft, while fully accepting that this was the politicisation of an essentially criminal phenomenon. He argues that the 'seminal causes' of each new phase of hijacking have been unsolved political problems, which the contemporary great powers either ignored or failed to address properly. This analysis leads him to conclude that solving the root problems of the Palestinians and improving US relations with Iran may go some way towards eradicating the scourge of aviation terrorism. Hence Peter St John's discussion, like Ariel Merari's, seeks to offer practical recommendations for the policy-maker in the light of his assessment of the threat.

In his review of aircraft sabotage, Brian Jenkins reminds us that the sabotage of passenger aircraft is one of the deadliest threats posed by contemporary terrorists. He records that since 1969 there have been more than 70 known attempts to plant bombs on board airliners, and these have caused 15 crashes in which 1,732 people have died. He points out that the terrorists' shift of emphasis from hijacking to sabotage bombing of airliners reflects a well-established terrorist trend 'toward large-scale indiscriminate violence', also mirrored, for example, in the tactic of using huge truck bombs in city centres.

In the introduction to his article on Aircraft Sabotage Brian Jenkins also explains some of the key factors which continue to make civil aviation such an attractive target for terrorists. It 'offers terrorists concentrations of people – mostly strangers – in enclosed environments, generally poses little security challenge and allows easy escape'. He also comments (see abstracts) that:

> commercial aviation historically has been a favourite target of terrorists who have viewed airliners as nationally-labelled containers of hostages in the case of hijackings, or victims in the case of sabotage.

One attraction of attacking civil aviation that seems to be missing from this list is the gaining of dramatic world-wide publicity. This was certainly important to groups such as the PFLP in their efforts to use hijackings in the early 1970s as a method of political extortion. However, as Brian Jenkins explains, few sabotage bombings of airliners:

> are credibly claimed by any terrorist group... the lack of claims may reflect the changing motives and organisational patterns of terrorism ... . Terrorists working on behalf of state sponsors, determined solely to punish their perceived enemies, or inspired by religious fanaticism with God or His self-appointed spokesperson as their sole constituent have no need to claim responsibility.

Newer and emerging threats to aviation security are not overlooked in this volume. Bruce Hoffman analyses the potential threat to air cargo integrators and concludes that while it cannot be entirely discounted:

> Terrorists have not attacked air cargo integrators because they lack ... identification or associational value, are considerably less well-known than commercial air passenger carriers, and since they do not carry passengers whose death and injury is grist for the media, do not have the same 'sensationalism', and publicity value as established passenger carriers.

In his review of the missile threat to civil aircraft Marvin B. Schaffer provides a balanced assessment of the threat, drawing attention to the proliferation of man-portable missiles and the increasing probability of terrorist groups not only acquiring some of these weapons but most probably also using them against civilian aircraft. He therefore argues that it is now in the public interest to develop a program to develop equipment to negate the threat of man-portable missiles and to stockpile it without waiting for a new catastrophic event to occur.

In his concluding essay, in addition to arguing the case for substantially strengthening the international civil aviation system against terrorism, Paul Wilkinson also briefly considers some of the ominous possibilities of terrorists using chemical, biological or radiological weapons or cyberwar against civil aviation. A key lesson that governments and the aviation security industry should have learned from Lockerbie is that we must never again allow our security to lag behind the tactics and weapons of the terrorists. His observation leads logically to the second part of this volume, which is concerned primarily with problems of international and national responses to the challenges of aviation terrorism.

* * *

Rodney Wallis contributes an illuminating and thought-provoking review of the role of the international organisations – ICAO, IATA, ECAC and ACI – in enhancing aviation security. Drawing upon his wealth of experience as director of security of IATA, he soon dispels the notion that their contribution is only of marginal value. He shows how all the major international aviation organizations 'working in partnership' have developed international conventions, standards, procedures and practices which all play a vital part in the strengthening of the global aviation security regime, despite the formidable obstacles inherent in the nature of modern international relations.

Brian Jenkins' second essay casts a critical though constructive eye over aviation security in the United States. As a member of the White House Commission on Aviation Safety and Security chaired by Vice President Gore, he is also able to provide an insight into how the Commission carried out its work, and assesses its impact on US aviation security policy and measures. Among the key policy issues he raises are unavoidable and crucial questions: who should pay for improvements in aviation security?; how can US aviation security be more effectively regulated and monitored to ensure that aviation security policy and the Gore Commission's key recommendations are properly implemented?

Omar Malik's parallel study of British aviation security against terrorism is equally critical and constructive, drawing valuably on the author's professional experience as a Captain in British Airways, as convener of the British Airline Pilots' Association security committee, and as a member of the National Aviation Security Committee, in addition to his academic knowledge. He concludes with a favourable overall assessment of Britain's track record, especially since Lockerbie, in pursuing higher aviation standards. However, he is highly critical of what he describes as 'Government unwillingness to contribute to the industry's costs ...' and .... 'its failure to develop a constructive partnership with industry'.

* * *

As the publication of this study of aviation terrorism and security has been timed to coincide with the tenth anniversary of the Lockerbie bombing, it is particularly appropriate that the volume contains an article by Dr Jim Swire on behalf of UK Families Flight 103. Dr Swire has been the tireless leader of the UK families group. Perhaps understandably, Jim Swire's article reflects the group's preoccupation with the effort to secure a trial of the two Libyan suspects indicted by the Scottish and American authorities in 1991 for their alleged role in the bombing. As the Libyan leader has steadfastly refused to hand them over to the US or British authorities, despite the UN sanctions aimed at forcing him to do so, Jim Swire (with the help of Professor Robert Black of Edinburgh University's law faculty and other indefatigable supporters, such as Tam Dalyell MP) has campaigned hard to get the British and American governments to allow a trial of the Lockerbie suspects in a neutral country under Scottish law. By mid-summer 1998 the British and American authorities had agreed to a proposal on these lines, and the Dutch government had given its approval to the idea of holding the trial in The Hague. In late August, Colonel Gadaffi appeared to agree in principle to such a trial, but a week later he made an announcement that seemed to reject the US–British proposal. At the time of going to press, it is difficult to tell whether Colonel Gadaffi's statement is simply a ploy to secure guarantees from Washington, London and The Hague that the two Libyan suspects will under no circumstances be extradited from Holland to the US or the UK, or is a complete reversal of his previous position. If the latter, Gadaffi's action is likely to deepen suspicion that the Libyan regime is afraid of a trial because it believes it has much to hide. If Colonel Gadaffi does finally reject the offer of a trial in the Netherlands, the US and UK governments will seek stronger UN sanctions against Libya for its refusal to hand over the Lockerbie suspects for trial, probably including an oil embargo. If, on the other hand, a trial does go ahead it will be an unique judicial process, conducted according to Scottish law but without a jury, and taking place in a foreign country.

It must be emphasised, however, that it is not the aim of the present volume to add to the mountain of theories and speculation about the criminal investigation into Lockerbie, though some of the major theories concerning the authorship of the crime are usefully surveyed by Peter St. John. In his concluding essay on enhancing global aviation security, Paul Wilkinson stresses the importance of judicial co-operation to bring those guilty of crimes of aviation terrorism to justice.

The editors share the view that everything must be done to secure a proper trial of the two Libyan suspects indicted for the Lockerbie bombing. A fair and thorough trial offers the only real prospect of discovering those responsible for authorizing, planning and carrying out this atrocity and ensuring that they are brought to justice. The fact that a decade has elapsed since Lockerbie makes the pursuit of the criminal investigation more difficult but by no means impossible. A success in bringing at least some of the individuals responsible for the Lockerbie bombing to justice would be a great victory for the international rule of law and might help to deter at least some of those who may be planning further atrocities.

However, the major emphasis of the contributors to *Aviation Terrorism and Security* is on reassessing the terrorist threat to civil aviation and reviewing the implications for aviation security policy, measures and procedures. If aviation security measures and procedures had been thoroughly implemented in the case of Pan Am 103, the perpetrators would never have succeeded in planting their bomb on board. Every time aviation security thwarts a sabotage bombing of a jumbo jet it saves hundreds of lives. The challenge discussed in this volume is how to improve not only our national airport and airline security systems, but how to ensure that all airline passengers and crew, regardless of their countries of origin and their destination, can enjoy the highest standards of international aviation security, matching the best practise in the major aviation countries.

The battle to protect civil aviation passengers and crew can only be won if the law-abiding members of the international community combine their efforts to tackle the scourge of international terrorism in all its forms. Our freedom of the airways is ultimately dependent on our ability to preserve the freedom of society as a whole. Dedicating ourselves to the vigorous pursuit of these goals would be the best memorial to the passengers and crew of Pan Am 103 and the many hundred of other innocent victims of aviation terrorism.

Paul Wilkinson
Brian M. Jenkins

2

Attacks On Civil Aviation:
Trends and Lessons

ARIEL MERARI

As we approach the end of the twentieth century, the threat to commercial aviation is no longer new. The basic modes of attack on aviation have not changed for years. The first terrorist hijacking for political extortion occurred in July 1968; the first terrorist bombing in mid-air of an airliner took place in May 1949, the first armed assault on an airliner on the ground occurred in June 1968, and the first indiscriminate armed assault on passengers at an airport happened in May 1972. Nearly three decades have passed during which effective countermeasures could be devised. The purpose of this paper is to survey the attributes of attacks on commercial aviation and, in particular, to examine the adequacy of the response to the threat.

For this endeavor an elaborate data base of attacks on commercial aviation was created, using a variety of sources. These included Tel Aviv University's Political Violence Research Unit data base on terrorism, FAA publications, ITERATE, Israel's Defense Forces' Spokesman's chronology, RAND-St Andrews University Chronology, CEDRE's chronology, as well as information found in articles and books.

For discerning the major trends, the fifty years between 1947 and 1996 was divided into five decades. The results of the analysis are presented below. The statistics do not include attacks on charter flights, general aviation aircraft, and military aircraft and airfields. They also do not include attacks on air crews outside the aircraft and the airport. They do include attacks on scheduled flights, on airports, and on commercial airline offices serving the general public, in time of peace (i.e., attacks in *de facto* war zones, such as in Bosnia during the civil war, were not included).

From the outset, it was clear that there is a great difference between attacks committed by individuals motivated by private, personal interests, and attacks perpetrated by politically motivated terrorist groups, state agents, and criminal organizations, such as drug traffickers. Organized groups have greater capabilities in terms of planning, number of assailants, weapons and explosives, reconnaissance, and determination. They also have an 'organizational memory'; they learn from experience. In many ways, they constitute the greatest threat to commercial aviation. For this reason, attacks by terrorist groups were analyzed separately, so as to compare them to the overall figures.

Frequency Of Attacks

The combined frequency of all attacks on commercial aviation in the five decades since 1947 is depicted in Figure 1. It is evident that attacks were quite rare before 1967. They rose sharply in the 1967–76 decade and reached a peak in the next decade. Although they declined by about 50 per cent in the recent decade (1987–96), they were still a widespread phenomenon.

FIGURE 1
TOTAL NUMBER OF ATTACKS PER DECADE ON COMMERCIAL AVIATION
1947–96

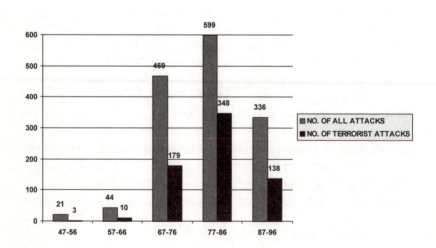

Types Of Attacks

Classified by target, attacks on commercial aviation can be carried out against airliners, airports, and airline offices. Whereas the data base is fairly comprehensive with regard to attacks on airliners and airports, coverage of attacks on airline offices is somewhat deficient, presumably because they are relatively inconspicuous in terms of media value. It is clear, however, that airliners have been by far the most common target for attacks on commercial aviation. During the entire 50-year period, there were 1,098 attacks on airliners, compared with 129 attacks on airports and 249 attacks on airline offices. Attacks on airports and airline offices are not committed by private persons. They are a tactic used by terrorist groups. Therefore, they only appeared in 1968, when international terrorism started rising.

Figure 2 shows the frequency of attacks on these three types of targets over the years, and Figure 3 shows the distribution of attacks on the three types of target throughout the entire period, comparing terrorist attacks with all attacks (terrorist and non-terrorist).

Another classification of attacks is by mode of operation. With regard to aviation, the main modes of operation are hijacking, bombing, and armed assaults. Other modes of attack comprised a negligible part of the incidents: there were five barricade-hostage events in airports and

FIGURE 2
NUMBER OF ATTACKS ON AIRLINERS, AIRPORTS, AND AIRLINE OFFICES
BY DECADE, 1947–96

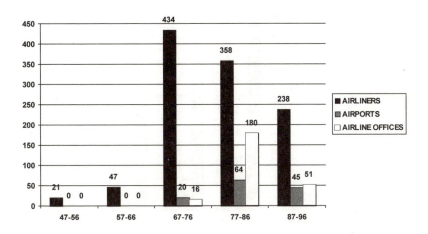

FIGURE 3
NUMBER OF ALL ATTACKS AND TERRORIST ATTACKS ON AIRLINERS,
AIRPORTS, AND AIRLINE OFFICES, 1947–96

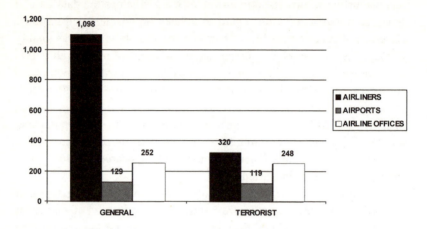

airline offices, 22 arson incidents, 12 cases of sabotage, and three letter bombs.

By far the most common form of attack on commercial aviation has been hijacking. This type of attack encompassed 959 incidents (65 per cent of all incidents) in the period of 1947–96. Hijackings constituted 87 per cent of all attacks on airliners (959 of 1,098 incidents). The other

FIGURE 4
FREQUENCY OF MAIN FORMS OF ATTACK ON AIRLINERS BY DECADE,
1947–96

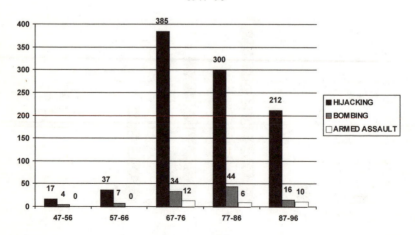

significant forms of attack on airliners were bombing (on the ground or in mid-flight) and armed assault (shooting at aircraft on the ground or in flight, throwing hand grenades, etc.). Figure 4 shows the distribution of the main forms of attack on airliners in the five decades.

All three major forms of attack on airliners display the same trend over time, rising steeply in the 1967-1976 decade, and then declining in the following two decades. It is important to note, however, that even in the recent decade, the rate of attacks is still quite high. The magnitude of the threat is still a reason for worry.

A look at the rate and composition of terrorist-perpetrated attacks against airliners over time shown in Figure 5, shows the same trend as for all perpetrators (terrorist and non-terrorist combined). Furthermore, a comparison of Figure 4 with Figure 5 shows that almost all of the bombings and armed assaults against airliners have been perpetrated by terrorist groups (86 per cent and 89 per cent, respectively).

FIGURE 5
FREQUENCY OF MAIN FORMS OF ATTACK ON AIRLINERS BY TERRORIST
GROUPS, 1947–96

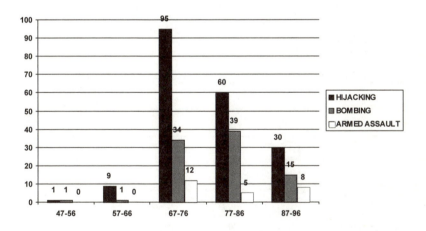

Presumably, the hijackers' purpose may influence the course and outcomes of the hijacking. Hijackers have had various objectives. Classification of hijackings by motivation is not always easy, and in some of the cases the available information is insufficient for identifying the hijackers' purpose. Nevertheless, an attempt has been made to analyze hijackings by the hijackers' objectives. Evaluation of the hijackers' motivation was possible in 854 cases of the 959 hijackings which occurred in the five decades under consideration. The predominant motivation has been 'escape'; i.e., merely to divert the airliner so as to arrive at another destination. Second in frequency is hijacking for extortion. In these cases the hijackers demand something in addition to mere travel to a certain place, and the implementation of their demands depends on governments' will, not on the airliner crew's co-operation. Some hijackings are done merely to express protest, with no demands attached. In these cases the hijackers do not explicitly threaten the hostages lives. Still other hijackings have been committed by mentally disturbed persons. In some of these cases the demands have been unclear, and in others they have been utterly bizarre and irrational. Figure 6 shows the frequency of the main motivations for hijacking, as a percentage of the cases in which the hijackers' objectives could be identified.

FIGURE 6
MOTIVATIONS FOR HIJACKINGS AS PERCENTAGE OF ALL HIJACKINGS, 1947–96

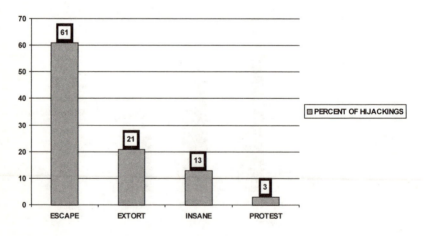

The distribution of objectives of hijackings committed by terrorist groups is significantly different from the general picture. This distribution is shown in Figure 7 for the 166 terrorist hijackings in which the hijackers' purpose could be identified.

FIGURE 7
MOTIVATIONS FOR HIJACKING AS PERCENTAGE OF ALL HIJACKINGS BY
TERRORIST GROUPS, 1947–96

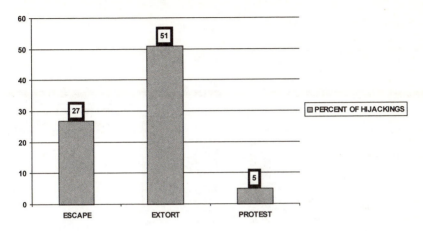

Unlike attacks on airliners, attacks on airports (bombing and armed assaults) peaked in the 1977–1986 decade. They also declined in the recent decade. Almost all attacks on airports were committed by terrorist groups, as shown in Figures 8 and 9.

FIGURE 8
BOMB ATTACKS ON AIRPORTS: ALL ATTACKS AND TERRORIST ATTACKS,
1947–96

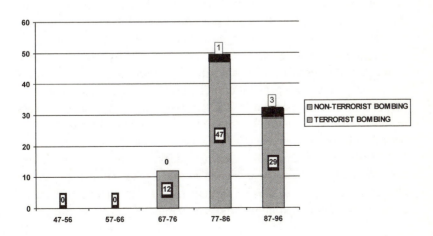

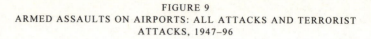

FIGURE 9
ARMED ASSAULTS ON AIRPORTS: ALL ATTACKS AND TERRORIST
ATTACKS, 1947–96

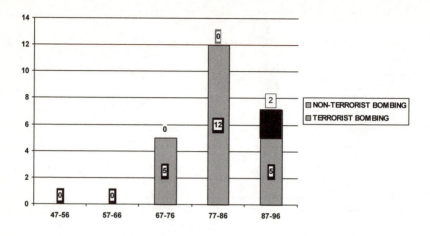

Casualties Of Attacks

The number of casualties resulting from attacks on commercial aviation
has increased steadily during the five decades. This fact is particularly
striking in view of the decline in the number of attacks during the most
recent two decades. In the last decade, fatalities increased by 26 per cent
compared to the previous decade, although the number of attacks
dropped by nearly 50 per cent. This means that, on average, attacks
have become increasingly lethal over the years. Figure 10 shows the
number of fatalities of attacks against aviation targets by decade.

   Almost all casualties have resulted from attacks by terrorist groups.
In the five decades under consideration the total number of fatalities
was 3,347. Eighty two per cent of them, or 2,752 people, died in attacks
perpetrated by terrorist groups. The terrorist share is particularly salient
in the last three decades: 98 per cent of all fatalities in the 1967–76
period, 98 per cent in the 1977–86 period, and 85 per cent in the
1987–96 period. Presumably, terrorist attacks are more lethal mainly
because many of them are designed to kill a large number of people
indiscriminately. These are, in particular, bombing attacks and armed
assaults. As mentioned above, most of the attacks in these categories

FIGURE 10
NUMBER OF FATALITIES IN ATTACKS AGAINST AVIATION TARGETS,
1947–96

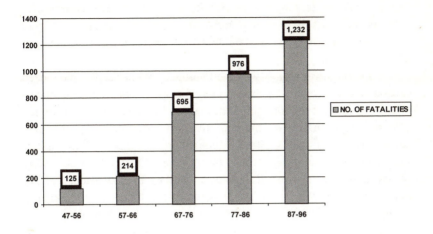

FIGURE 11
NUMBER OF FATALITIES IN TERRORIST GROUPS' ATTACKS AGAINST
AVIATION TARGETS, 1947–96

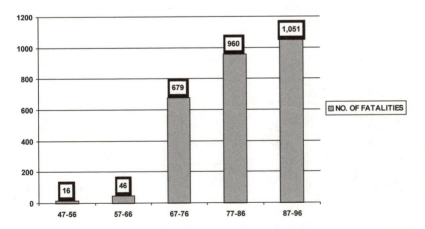

have been perpetrated by terrorist groups rather than by unorganized individuals. Furthermore, terrorist groups have greater capabilities than private persons, which result in greater fire power. By and large, therefore, the history of the development of the threat to commercial aviation is the history of modern terrorism, its tactics and targets. Figure 11 portrays the number of fatalities of terrorist groups' attacks on aviation over the years.

By far, the great majority of the fatalities – 93 per cent – have been caused in attacks against airliners. Only 5 per cent resulted from attacks in airports and 2 per cent from attacks on airline companies' offices.
The relative lethality of the various forms of attack has differed according to the target. In attacks against airliners most of the fatalities were caused by bombing (nearly 74 per cent). Nineteen per cent were caused in hijacking, most of them as a result of an inadvertent crash of the airliner following a shoot-out between the hijackers and security guards; 7 per cent were caused by armed assaults on airliners.

Fatalities in attacks on airports were about evenly caused by armed assaults (51 per cent) and bombings (49 per cent).

Most of the fatalities in attacks on airline offices were caused by bombing (91 per cent). Only 9 per cent resulted from armed assaults.

Further analysis of these results, therefore, shows that the majority (almost 69 per cent) of all fatalities in attacks against aviation have been

FIGURE 12
PERCENTAGE OF FATALITIES OF BOMBINGS ON AIRLINERS OUT OF ALL
FATALITIES IN ATTACKS AGAINST AVIATION TARGETS, 1947–96

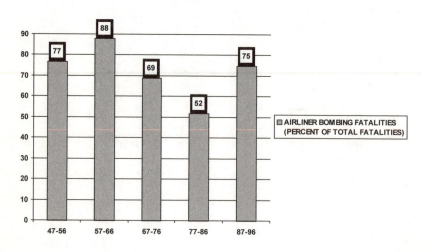

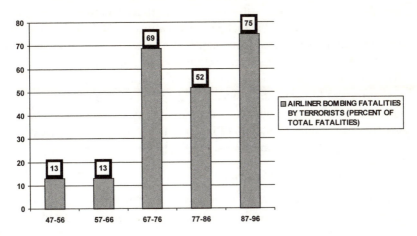

FIGURE 13
PERCENTAGE OF FATALITIES OF TERRORIST BOMBINGS ON AIRLINERS
OUT OF ALL FATALITIES IN ATTACKS AGAINST AVIATION TARGETS,
1947–96

caused in bombings on board airliners. Figure 12 shows the percentage of fatalities caused by bombs on airliners, out of all fatalities, over the years.

Narrowing down the types of attacks which caused casualties still further, reveals that the majority of the fatalities have been the result of bombing attacks against airliners perpetrated by terrorist groups. Fifty-nine per cent of all fatalities in the whole period under consideration were the result of this particular source. The distribution by decade is shown in Figure 13.

Effectiveness Of Security Measures

A great effort has been invested over the years, particularly since 1968, in devising security measures to prevent attacks on commercial aviation. The three-decade perspective warrants an examination of the effectiveness of these measures. The basic method used here for this purpose is an analysis of the rate of foiled attacks in the various categories. The rationale of using the rate of thwarting as a criterion for security measures' effectiveness is simple: in a hypothetical case of perfect security measures, all attempted attacks would be foiled and the rate of thwarting would, therefore, be 100 per cent. Conversely, in a hypothetical case of a total failure of the security system, all attempted attacks would succeed and the rate of foiling would, therefore, be 0 per cent. Moreover, it could be expected that the rate of thwarting would increase over the years, with the accumulation of experience of the threat. Indeed, it is arguable that part of the utility of the security system is in its deterrence value. Hence, not only the rate of thwarting should serve as a measure of effectiveness, but also the rate of trying to attack. As much as this assertion is plausible, it is still true that, in the last count, the test of the security system is in coping with those that are not deterred. Furthermore, changes in the frequency of attempted attacks may be attributable to a variety of factors, such as the political situation, in addition to the deterrence impact of the physical security system.

The Rate of Thwarting Hijackings

A stringent criterion was used for assessing the thwarting of a hijacking attempt. An attempt to hijack an airliner was considered thwarted only if the hijackers did not manage to gain control of the aircraft for any length of time. Thus, the incident was not considered thwarted, even if the hijackers were eventually subdued by the crew or passengers or the aircraft landed in its original destination despite the hijacking. The reason for using this strict criterion is that the security system is supposed to prevent access to the aircraft of the would-be hijacker so that he is not able to seize control (for example, before boarding), and to prevent the would-be hijacker from obtaining, either on board or in the vicinity of the aircraft, the means to effect the hijacking and, if these fail, at least to prevent him from actually seizing control of the airliner. Sufficient information for determining whether or not the attempted hijacking was foiled could be found for 943 of the 959 hijacking incidents which occurred in the recent 50 years. Of these, 296 hijacking attempts (31 per cent) were foiled.

The rate of thwarting hijackings perpetrated by terrorist groups is considerably lower than the general rate of thwarting. Of the 193 hijacking incidents committed by terrorist groups in the 50 year period, for which there was information for determining whether or not they were foiled, only 36 attempted hijackings were thwarted (19 per cent). The lower rate of thwarting of terrorist hijacking can be explained by the greater professionalism and tenacity of terrorist groups compared to the occasional, personally-motivated individual. The greater number of hijackers that is characteristic of terrorist hijackings, their superior weapons and better planning, make it much more difficult to hinder a terrorist hijacking once the hijackers gained access to the airliner. Yet, in cases where the terrorists gain access to the airliner through the normal boarding routine (and this is by far the most common case), the non-terrorist hijacker may have an advantage in evading detection.

Figure 14 shows the rate of foiling of all hijackings and terrorist hijackings for each decade.

FIGURE 14
PERCENTAGE OF FOILED HIJACKINGS OUT OF THE TOTAL NUMBER OF
ATTEMPTS, 1947–96

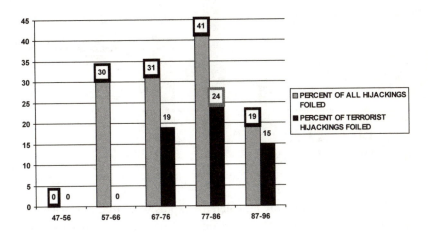

Figure 14 shows that despite the accumulated experience and the investment in aviation security, the rate of thwarting hijackings has not improved significantly since this phenomenon became a major problem thirty years ago.

The Rate of Thwarting Bombing of Airliners

As has been indicated above, bombs on airliners caused most of the fatalities of attacks against commercial aviation. It is therefore of great interest to examine the rate of foiling of this mode of attack. The criterion for thwarting in this category of attack was simple: an incident was considered thwarted whenever the explosive device was discovered and rendered harmless before it exploded or before it was designed to explode. The cases in which the failure to explode was due to malfunctioning of the explosive device were not regarded as thwarting.

Over the years, only 18 of the 106 cases of bombing of airliners have been foiled (17 per cent). Figure 15 shows the rate of thwarting for each decade.

FIGURE 15
PERCENTAGE OF FOILED BOMBING OF AIRLINERS OUT OF THE TOTAL
NUMBER OF ATTEMPTS, 1947–96

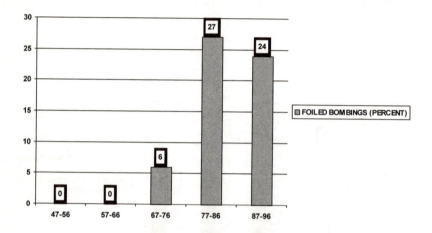

Information on the way in which the explosive charge was placed on the airliner was known to me in only 32 of the cases in which the bombing was not foiled. In 11 cases the bomb was brought on board by an unwitting passenger; in nine of the cases the bomb was brought on board by passengers who disembarked and left the bomb to explode later; in eight cases the bomb was in a piece of luggage which was checked in for a flight, but the person who checked it in did not board the flight ('no show'); in three cases the bomb was in an air mail parcel which arrived on board through the postal service; and in two cases the bomb was apparently smuggled to the aircraft by ground personnel.

In the cases where a bombing on an airliner was foiled, it is of interest to know how the bomb was detected. Information was available for 16 of the 18 thwarted bombings. In 10 of them the explosive charge was found in a routine security check before boarding; in four additional cases intelligence information led to the discovery of the bomb; and in two cases the bomb was discovered incidentally by a steward.

Conclusions and Recommendations

Despite the long-accumulated experience with attacks on commercial aviation, and notwithstanding the immense investment in security measures and procedures, the effectiveness of aviation security measures has not improved during the past three decades. In the recent decade, the average hijacker had an 81 per cent chance of actually seizing control of the airliner. The terrorist hijacker had an even higher chance of success – 85 per cent. The rate of success in bombing attacks against airliners, the principal cause of death in attacks on commercial aviation, has also been appallingly high – 76 per cent.

One might imagine that these worldwide figures do not reflect the security level in Western countries, where awareness is higher, security procedures are more strictly enforced, and security-related technology is more readily available. Not quite so. Indeed, in North America the rate of thwarting of hijackings over the most recent two decades has been 43 per cent and in Western Europe 24 per cent (still, a better than two-to-one and three-to-one chance of success for the average hijacker, respectively). Yet, in the most recent decade the thwarting rate in North America has dropped to 23 per cent and in Western Europe to merely 8 per cent. The rate of foiling of bombing of airliners also leaves much to be desired. In North America it was 22 per cent over the most recent two decades (only two of nine bombing attacks were foiled), and in Western Europe, 60 per cent (nine of 15 bombing attacks were foiled).

To some extent, the low rate of thwarting hijackings is a matter of policy, rather than capability. In many cases the hijackers did not have real weapons, and succeeded in their venture only because it is the policy of some airline companies and governments to treat any hijacker who waves a wrapped parcel claiming that it contains a bomb as if he has a real explosive device. Of the 151 cases in which the hijackers had fake weapons, or claimed to have weapons but did not display them, only 34 per cent were thwarted.

Notwithstanding these partial explanations, the blunt fact is that the effort to protect commercial aviation from attacks has by and large failed. The failure is especially remarkable because the problem is quite specific and circumscribed. Most of the casualties result from attacks on airliners, which are a distinct target that can conceivably be fully protected: the physical area of an airliner is enclosed and access to it is controlled. Unlike airports and airline offices, which are open to the general public and commonly accessible, approach and entry to an airliner can be subjected to strict scrutiny. As it is quite clear that the failure of security is not the result of continuous, widespread negligence or indifference of security personnel, the reasons for the poor results should be sought in the basic approach to the problem. These fundamental causes are briefly discussed below.

Lack of Foresight

A look at the history of attacks on commercial aviation reveals that new terrorist methods of attack have virtually never been foreseen by security authorities. The security system was caught by surprise when an airliner was first hijacked for political extortion; it was unprepared when an airliner was attacked on the tarmac by a terrorist team firing automatic weapons; when terrorists, who arrived as passengers, collected their luggage from the conveyer belt, took out weapons from their suitcases, and strafed the crowd in the arrival's hall; when a parcel bomb sent by mail exploded in an airliner's cargo hold in mid-flight; when a bomb was brought on board by an unwitting passenger, and so on. True, once terrorists used a new tactic or introduced a technical innovation the aviation security complex usually adapted its procedures fairly rapidly, so as to close the hole in the system. But the terrorists have not been torpid. They have looked for new ways to circumvent the security system. And, since some terrorist groups have capable and innovative operatives and some enjoy direct access to sponsor-states' capabilities, it did not take long before they originated a new method of attack. Thus, the history of attacks on aviation is the chronicle of a cat-and-mouse game, where the cat is busy blocking old holes and the mouse always succeeds in finding new ones.

It is easy to recommend foresight, but practically impossible to implement it in a satisfactory manner. Moreover, no matter how innovative security personnel are, there is no guarantee that they will always outsmart the adversary. The solution, therefore, should be sought elsewhere. At present, the aviation security system relies on a combination of two components: passenger screening, designed to identify the would-be hijacker or bomb-carrier; and x-ray machines designed to identify the weapons and explosives. In fact, either one of the two components would suffice, had it been perfect. Theoretically, if it is certain that no assailant or unwitting bomb carrier is on board, it is unnecessary to bother looking for weapons, and if there is certainty that no weapons or explosives are on board, it is unnecessary to look for assailants. The problem is that at present neither of the two components in the system, nor both in combination, provide the necessary certainty. It is better to concentrate an effort to make one perfect screening method instead of two partially effective ones. In the choice between investment in developing perfect passenger screening procedures and investment in developing a perfect weapons and explosives detection device, the latter is much more promising. There is practically no hope that passenger profiling may reach 100 per cent accuracy. Bombs have occasionally been smuggled even on board El Al airliners, an airline company known for its emphasis on an elaborate and thorough passenger-profile security system.

Inherent Limitations of an Airline Companies'-Based Security System

Is the aviation security system professional? Naturally, there are differences between countries, airports, and airline companies. In general, however, wherever the responsibility is passed to the airline company, security cannot be expected to be truly professional. Airline companies do not have, nor can they obtain on a regular basis, the capabilities that are essential to cope effectively with sophisticated terrorist groups or state terrorism. These capabilities pertain to several aspects of security. Knowledge of terrorist modes of operation, terrorists' psychological and demographic profiles, terrorist groups' intentions and concrete plans for attacks, details of terrorist weapons and explosive devices and methods of concealing and smuggling them, technical innovations and preparations by terrorist groups and their sponsor states, the whereabouts of terrorist operatives, their aliases, travel documents in their use – all these are a specialty of governments' intelligence services. Commercial companies do not have the knowledge and expertise; nor do they have the access to intelligence sources which are essential for monitoring terrorist threats. It can be argued that government intelligence agencies can pass this information to airline companies on a need-to-know basis. Such a procedure, however, cannot work well. Intelligence agencies tend to be very careful in sharing information, especially with organizations outside the government system that are not subject to security classification reviews and are not bound by government regulations and penalties for unauthorized dissemination of information. Furthermore, the working relations between government agencies and airline companies are inherently more awkward than the inter-agency communication which exists between government organizations, which is facilitated by bureaucratic links and normal working routines and procedures.

Commercial companies also do not have ready access to the qualified personnel needed to perform counter-terrorism duties, nor are they capable of training such personnel. Only government security agencies can accomplish these requirements.

A thorough implementation of aviation security measures involves a very heavy financial burden. The cost of selecting, training and employing qualified security personnel is high. The purchase, maintenance and operation of the increasingly sophisticated screening equipment is also expensive. In the highly competitive business environment of the air transportation industry, carrying the cost of security in the manner that it should be done may bring even a large airline company to bankruptcy.

For all these reasons, to put the burden of security on the shoulders of airline companies is bureaucratically an easy solution, which is a recipe for the perpetuation of the existing unsatisfactory state of affairs. Governments must recognize their comprehensive responsibility for aviation security and shoulder this task.

So far I have discussed aviation security from the narrow perspective of defensive measures. However, in view of the fact that most of the casualties are caused by terrorists rather than by common criminals or the insane, there is a broader political-strategic aspect that must not be neglected. Terrorism is a form of warfare, which is directed against the state rather than against any particular commercial company. Airliners and airline companies are chosen by terrorists as targets partly because they constitute symbols of states. Unlike a 'private', individual hijacker, a terrorist group is usually a known organization, which has bases and offices. This is certainly true in the case of state terrorism, where attacks are committed by agents of foreign governments. Under these circumstances, measures to prevent attacks on aviation must not be limited to physical defense. The government must take steps to deter the terrorists and sponsoring states by all means at its disposal. This important aspect merits a separate discussion, which is beyond the scope of this paper.

The text of this article is based on a lecture given at the White House Commission – GWU Conference on Aviation Safety in the Twenty-First Century. Thanks are due to Emmanuel ('Mike') Ackerman, President of the Ackerman Group, for his useful advice and commentary.

3

The Politics of Aviation Terrorism

PETER ST. JOHN

Of the available forms of theater, few are so captivating figuratively, as well as literally, as skyjacking. The boldness of the action, the obviousness of the danger, the numbers of people involved as hostages and therefore potential victims, the ease with which national boundaries can be traversed and international incidents created, the instantaneous radio and television linkages, all these combine to make this crime one of the most immediately attractive forms of terrorist action.[1]

With these words Jan Schreiber summarizes the most spectacular aspect of international terrorism – hijacking. Hijacking is, in at least one respect, unique in the catalogue of criminal activities in that 'no other crime in the world can pick itself up, its perpetrators and its victims, and move them from point to point at just under the speed of sound'.[2]

The hijacking of modern commercial jets creates a special form of theatre in which notions of spectacle, fear, excitement and communication are all concentrated inside the hull of one aircraft. Airport property, or even the plane itself, may be blown up. Human lives may be threatened or taken. Backed by periodic torture or even killings, threats may be used to extort money, or to obtain the release of prisoners, the publication of manifestos, or safe conduct to another country far from the scene of the crime. The actors include the terrorists themselves, governments, the victims, the media and public opinion and, in this way, hijacking mimics other forms of terrorism, for at the heart of the process is the confrontation between terrorists and governments. Terrorists propose to move, change, destabilize or destroy governments by provoking an intemperate government response to their seizure or murder of innocent hostages. Knowing this, one might think the response of nation states to terrorist attacks on their own citizens and on civil aviation generally would be immediate and decisive, but this has not been the case. In fact, the exercise of state sovereignty against hijack terrorists has been a highly political process.

In the first place, governments rarely implement preventive measures that anticipate future terrorist attacks. Thus states are nearly always unprepared and forced by such attacks into a reactive stance, often failing to learn the lessons of proactivity from neighbouring states that have endured a terrorist siege. Secondly, states insist on retaining sovereign control over their responses to terrorism and refuse to yield pride of place to the obvious need for international co-operation and response. Thirdly, preoccupied with the business of governing, democratic states often find that their enthusiasm for further, possibly expensive, preventive action, quickly dissipates after the initial surprise of a terrorist attack. Thus it is only after a real disaster or a sustained series of attacks that democracies take serious action. Finally, democratic governments are quite capable of deviousness when faced with terrorist ultimatums. As Geoffrey Lipman, former Director General of the Geneva-based International Foundation of Airline Passengers Association (IFAPA), has said, 'It's hard to avoid cynicism when exposed to the daily farce of governments condemning terrorism and dealing covertly with terrorists – or the head of state calling for the death sentence for hijackers one day and repositioning himself the next, after a discussion with friendly foreign interests.'[3] In short, it has been hard for democracies to learn the lesson that terrorist attacks are not aimed at citizens, they are aimed at states.

As a criminal phenomenon, hijacking concerns the international community because unlawful interference with civil aviation hampers the normal free flow of air traffic and jeopardizes the freedom and lives of citizens of many different countries.[4] So hijacking is both criminal in nature and international in scope, but it is also frequently a political act. As Claude Bergeron writes: 'In many cases the assaults take on a significance that extends beyond the common criminal act. In fact they become a weapon wielded by political groups or warring countries. Since 1930, at least 600 assaults have been forms of pressure exerted for political dividends by persons or groups seeking to air their opinions.'[5]

My intention in this analysis is to explore the notion of political causation as a major cause of hijacking's enduring high profile, focusing on attacks on airports and sabotage of civil aircraft. Frequently, the issue of aircraft and airport security is treated as a technical problem with largely technical solutions. Just develop the right technology, say the security people, and the problem of hijacking will disappear.

In an earlier analysis of government responses to hijacking between 1968 and 1988, I extracted a list of 110 internationally significant hijacks from the 800 or 900 carried out during the period. I found that 91 of the 110 were aimed at 16 Western or Western-oriented countries. They were: Austria, Belgium, Canada, France, Greece, Holland, India, Israel, Italy, Japan, Kuwait, Malta, Switzerland, the UK, the USA, and West Germany.[6]

In that study I found a clear-cut distinction between soft-line and hard-line responses to terrorist hijacks. The soft-line approach was embraced by Austria, Belgium, Cyprus, Egypt, Greece, Italy, Japan, Malta, Pakistan, Spain and Thailand. The hard line approach came from Britain*, Canada, France*, Holland*, India, Israel, Jordan*, Kuwait*, South Korea, the USA and West Germany*. The countries marked with an asterisk changed from a soft- to a hard-line policy in the period under study. Using Bowyer Bell's categorization of government policies, I then developed a spectrum of government response to hijacking moving from hard-line to soft-line as follows: Retaliation, No Compromise, Flexibility, and Concession and Accommodation.[7]

By 1988 governments were in a position regarding hijacks as illustrated in Table 1:

TABLE 1
GOVERNMENT RESPONSES TO AVIATION TERRORISM

Retaliation	No Compromise	Flexibility	Concession and Accommodation
Israel	Britain	Belgium	Austria
U.S.	France *	Canada	Cyprus
	Holland*	Egypt *	Greece
	India*	Sweden	Italy
	Jordan*	Switzerland	Japan
	Kuwait*		Malta
	South Korea		Spain
	West Germany*		Thailand

* Indicates that by 1988 certain states appear to have moved from one category to another, usually in a hard-line direction.[8]

Looking back now over thirty years it is possible to see that the politicization of an essentially criminal phenomenon was fostered by a number of different factors. These included: domestic press coverage, which was largely unhelpful because it actually encouraged the committing of hijacks; the indulgence of the public, which tended to lionize the hijackers' criminal activity, and the capitulation of governments to the orders of assailants, which simply encouraged more terrorism. The submissiveness of airlines and their crews made it easy for criminals and mentally unbalanced people to hijack planes. The lack of preventive measures was another sign of the weakness of governments, which assumed the problem would go away. The existence of sanctuary states greatly weakened the international response to hijacking and gave comfort and encouragement to the hijackers; Algiers and Beirut spring to mind. States also became entangled by the contradiction of being caught between the long-term interest of combating unlawful interference and the short-term interest of extricating themselves from difficult situations at least cost. Not only do democratic governments change every few years, but parties of the left, right or centre come to power with a range of attitudes towards terrorist activity. Finally, governments failed to prosecute, sending a message to terrorists that they could safely get away with criminal acts, whether or not they were hiding behind a political purpose. As Bergeron has pointed out: 'none of these attitudes fostered a climate conducive to fighting this form of crime'.[9] The evolution of hijacking was also encouraged by the Cold War, which effectively blocked full international co-operation against terrorist hijacking, provided safe havens for terrorists and created non-western alternative sources of arms and weapons.

In spite of these setbacks, mistakes and wrong turns, the international civil aviation community has developed an impressive system of defences against hijacking. The International Civil Aviation Organization (ICAO) and the International Air Transport Association (IATA) spearheaded the process with the addition of the Airports Association Council International (AACI) in 1992. In a chapter entitled 'The Organizations' in *Combatting Air Terrorism* (1993), former IATA Security Chief Rodney Wallis brilliantly portrays the impact of the Bonn Declaration and Annex 17, the Security Advisory Committee of IATA, the Federal Aviation Authority (FAA) and the European Civil Aviation Conference (ECAC).[10] These measures were aimed at resisting the 'normal' process of hijacking, but in the late 1980s an abnormal political situation was facing the West.

This paper will analyze the essentially political nature of hijacking by demonstrating how several important political problems in the Middle East have coalesced and become internationalized through attacks on international civil aviation.[11] The problems are now 30 years old and the spin-offs from these seminal causes have spawned further series of hijacks in typical copycat fashion, giving the illusion of a monolithic attack on the West. As we shall see, each new phase of hijacking has been created by an unsolved political problem, which the contemporary great powers either ignored or failed to properly address.

The longer an internationalized political problem persists unsolved, the more desperate hijackers become. Sometimes disparate political protest groups co-operate or share their destructive expertise and such developments can be devastating for an apparatus as fragile as the international civil aviation community. In 1988, a truly significant milestone was reached with the destruction of Pan Am 103. As Rodney Wallis has written: 'The destruction of Pan Am 103 was an incident destined to have major repercussions on civil aviation operations.'[12] So too, he might have added, on governments. After outlining the clearly political origins of modern hijacking, I intend to demonstrate through a case study how the secret agendas of governments, the failure to address pressing international problems, and the evasion of agreed-upon international legal norms are seriously undermining the future safety of the international civil aviation regime.

The Politics of Hijacking

In order to understand the politics of contemporary international hijacking it is necessary to analyze the twin problems of the Palestinian question and the Iranian Revolution. Over a number of years, both the Palestinians and the Iranians developed a seething anger at the West, both for its intervention in their region and for its support for their enemies. One of the few ways of hitting back effectively was to strike at the vulnerable Western system of civil aviation in the form of hijacking.

In the select list of 110 major hijack episodes referred to above it is instructive to note that 47 hijack incidents are related to the Palestinian cause, 15 are related to Hizbollah (Iran) and 11 pertain to the Sikhs.

Thus in the 20-year period between 1968 and 1988, 74 of 110 hijacks emerged from the Middle East and West Asia. Not only did this cause much fear and enormous disruption, but it had the potential to induce Western states to change their polices *vis-à-vis* the Middle East. In fact, hijacking in the modern sense was the brainchild of Dr. George Habash, a Palestinian medical doctor and leader of the PFLP, the Popular Front for the Liberation of Palestine.

Ten years after Raoul Castro had used hijacking to disrupt communications within Cuba, Habash conceived the idea of shooting up El Al's B707s as a way of attacking Israel. But by turning passengers into hostages, blowing them out of the sky, and attacking them in the terminals, he went farther than Raoul Castro had in using it as political blackmail.[13]

Beginning in 1979, various factions of the Iranian Revolution connected to Lebanon also developed hijacking as a means of bringing about political change. Two overlapping lists of political events follow, which directly stimulated many among the long list of hijacks mentioned above.

The Palestinians
1. The Six Day War, 1967.
2. The Munich Olympics attack, 1972
3. The OPEC oil minister's kidnap, 1975
4. The Algiers hijack & Entebbe raid, 1976
5. The Camp David agreements, 1978
6. The Reagan assassination attempt, 1981
7. The Israeli invasion of Lebanon, 1982
8. The attack on the Achille Lauro, 1985

The Iranians
1.The Iranian Revolution, 1979
2. The Israeli invasion of Lebanon, 1982
3. Expulsion of the MNF from Lebanon, 1983
4. The Iranian hostages (Iran-Contra), 1985–86
5. The Air Arrow Gander explosion, 1985
6. The bombing of Libya, 1986
7. Iranian airbus shot down, 1988
8. The Pan Am 103 explosion, 1988

In order to understand the impact of terrorist hijacks on governmental response it is necessary to integrate the above political event list into the list of hijacks and then to juxtapose these two onto the different phases through which terrorism has developed during the period of study. In my book, *Air Piracy, Airport Security and International Terrorism* (1991), I pointed out that since its inception hijacks have followed a fairly predictable pattern of intensity followed by hiatus.

This pattern made hijacking more predictable for governments but they, in turn, made the mistake of miscalculating the dangerous increase in lethality of terrorist attacks. As a result of the failure to appreciate the political nature of hijacks, governments have been tempted to ignore security warnings and to indulge in cover-ups. An updated picture of these periods of intensity and hiatus follows:

1. 1947–52: Eastern Europeans escaping Communism;
2. 1952–58: Hiatus period, propeller to jet age;
3. 1958–61: Raoul Castro initiates hijacking in Cuba;
4. 1962–67: Hiatus period;
5. 1968–72: Palestinian skyjacking, hijacks to Cuba and criminals and psychotics in US;
6. 1973–78: Hiatus period as the West fights back;
7. 1979–88: Religious fundamentalist attacks by Arab, Iranian and Sikh groups plus Arab radicals;
8. 1989– : Hiatus period with fewer hijacks though some in Russia and Asia.

The period 1968-72 evinced an extraordinary resurgence of hijack aggression during which there were '396 incidents of unlawful interference, including 181 successful aircraft hijacks and 114 failed attempts'.[14] As Claude Bergeron further points out, 188 cases or 47 per cent of these were driven by non-political motives, while 181 cases or 46 per cent were driven by political motives. In Western Europe and the Middle East there was an extraordinary outburst of hijack terrorism as a result of Palestinian despair after the defeat of the Arab states in the 1967 war in the Middle East. Palestinian doctors George Habash and Waddi Haddad masterminded a sustained attack on Western civil aviation, which provoked the now-familiar airport security systems as well as the Tokyo (1963), Hague (1970) and Montreal Conventions (1971) internationally.

In 1973 the USA and Cuba signed a memorandum of understanding on hijacking of aircraft and vessels and other offences that helped regulate an unhappy relationship. During this period governments learned some basic lessons about defence against terrorist hijack attacks, but little about their political motivation.

The Munich Olympics attack on 5 September 1972 was a further political statement by the Palestinian Black September Organization (BSO) that reached millions of people all over the world, in addition to causing the death of 11 Israeli athletes. Three years later the

Palestinians made another political statement when Carlos the Jackal kidnapped OPEC oil ministers from their meeting in Vienna and abducted them to Algiers. The joint Baader Meinhof-PFLP hijack of an Air France airbus to Entebbe in Uganda on 27 June 1976 echoed the Palestinian intent. But the Israeli rescue of 100 Jewish passengers served to introduce a Western response phase of liberating hijacked planes with elite anti-terrorist groups. The rescue of a Lufthansa airliner at Mogadishu in October 1976 by a joint German and British operation emphasized this Western tendency.

Finally, the Camp David Agreements between President Carter, President Sadat and Prime Minister Begin in 1978 appeared at last to be addressing the Palestinian political problem. But soon this agreement was widely rejected by radical governments and groups all over the Middle East. After the Israeli invasion of Lebanon in 1982, many groups including the Palestinian Liberation Organization, Hizbollah, the Syrians and the Iranians all had yet another grievance against the West. In the mid-1980s the Abu Nidal organization, an extreme splinter group of the PLO, unleashed a devastating series of attacks on Western civil aviation at Malta, Cyprus, Rome and Vienna airports and Karachi. These attacks were calculated for maximum destruction of airline systems and created widespread fear of flying among the travelling public. Western airport security was still extremely porous as one successful attack after another demonstrated. Also the Abu Nidal group, in particular, seemed unconcerned about loss of life among its own members.

It would be helpful in hindsight to be able to say that the Abu Nidal group was the last gasp of Palestinian terrorism, but unfortunately an offshoot of the PFLP, the PFLP-GC or General Command under Ahmed Jibril, had become proficient at manufacturing bombs with timers which could also be pressure-detonated inside commercial aircraft. The use of Semtex plastic explosive for these bombs made them largely undetectable by traditional airport baggage inspection systems. And so almost inevitably the Palestinians joined forces with the Iranians to inflict a savage blow on the flagship US airline carrier – Pan American Airlines.

Meanwhile, the Iranian Revolution of 1979 brought to power a vengeful regime determined to use terrorism as state policy. Iran was equally prepared to intervene in Lebanon on behalf of its Shiite co-religionists, who had been invaded and dispersed by the Israeli invasion of 1982. Nearly 20 years later, it is still difficult to estimate the full extent of terrorist damage inflicted by the group alternately called Islamic Jihad or Hizbollah: The Party of God.

In 1982 and 1983, a Western multi-national peacekeeping force that included the USA was forced out of Lebanon by a series of deadly suicide bomb attacks. Soon after, Hizbollah was involved in the seizure of Western hostages in Beirut and a lengthy and agonizing saga ensued for the West. The seizure of hostages placed huge emotional pressure on the victim governments and led the latter to conclude secret deals with terrorist-sponsoring governments in order to retrieve the hostages. In the Iran-Contra deal, the Reagan administration exchanged arms for hostages, with the proceeds being funnelled to an illegal US covert operation in Nicaragua. Not surprisingly, this set the scene for government cover-ups and dishonesty.

According to Bob Woodward, in his book *Veil,* a restricted inter-agency group operating 'offshore' through the CIA was willing to buy the freedom of hostages with arms deals, made secretly with governments with which the USA had no official relations. At the same time the USA began supporting Iraq, which it had consistently declared to be a terrorist-sponsoring government. American arms flowed to Iraq throughout the latter part of the Iran-Iraq War, between 1980 and 1988.

Meanwhile, in December 1983, the Lebanese Hizbollah group in collusion with the Iranian government attempted a *coup* in Kuwait. In spite of multiple bomb explosions and considerable effort, the *coup* failed and 18 Iraqi-born Shiite conspirators were imprisoned as a result. Imad Mughniyah, a Lebanese Shiite whose brother-in-law was among the 18 prisoners in Kuwait, decided to mastermind a series of hijacks of Kuwaiti aircraft in order to free his brother-in-law.[15] In December 1984, a major hijack, the fourth by Mughniyah, resulted in the murder of two US overseas aid workers and the wounding of two Kuwaitis. Hizbollah next hijacked TWA 847 on a flight out of Athens, sending it back and forth between Beirut and Algiers for 14 days in June 1985. TWA 847 was a huge embarrassment for the Americans, but the principal demand was still the release of the 18 prisoners in Kuwait.

On 5 April 1988, a Kuwait airways B747, flying between Bangkok and Kuwait, was hijacked, diverted to Mashaad in Iran, then Cyprus and finally Algiers. Again hostages were shot, and members of the Kuwaiti royal family were terrorized in a hijack that lasted for a record 16 days. During this marathon Iran clearly favoured, encouraged and enabled the hijackers, while the US government was solidly in support of Kuwait. The standoff gave Iran an addition reason to despise the Kuwaiti government, which was already loathed for bringing US naval power into the Persian Gulf to protect Kuwait's oil shipments.

It was this US presence in the Gulf that eventually led to the most chilling episode in the history of hijacking: the explosion aboard Pan Am 103 in December 1988. It all began with the *USS Vincennes* on duty in the Persian Gulf.

Pan Am 103: A Case Study in Government Intrigue

On 21 December 1988, Pan Am 103 departed from Heathrow airport in London bound for New York and Detroit. The Boeing 747 carried 259 passengers, many of whom were Americans going home for Christmas. Less than 40 minutes into the flight, the 747 mysteriously exploded over Lockerbie, Scotland, ending the lives of all passengers and crew aboard the plane, along with 11 citizens of Lockerbie. This initiated one of the largest international counter-terrorist investigations ever undertaken. On the tenth anniversary of this wanton act of lawlessness there is still no consensus as to its perpetrator, though the US government and Scottish investigators named Libya in 1991.

The Libyans as Fall Guys

In November 1991, two Libyans, Abd al-Basit al-Meghrahi, a senior Libyan intelligence official, and Lamen Fhimah, the former manager of the Libyan Arab Airlines (LAA) office of Malta, were charged with carrying out the attack.[16] These two men were accused of placing a bomb aboard Pan Am 103 by obtaining and attaching an appropriately marked Air Malta tag to a suitcase that circumvented baggage security measures by routing the bag containing the bomb from Malta to Heathrow via Frankfurt. The evidence for this judgement is strongly circumstantial, mirroring a long history of Libyan-US hostilities since the early 1980s.

The US indictment stated that the two men placed a large, brown, hard-sided Samsonite suitcase on board Air Malta 180. On 7 December 1988 someone resembling al-Meghrahi had bought several items from a Maltese clothing store. The two arrived in Malta on 20 December with the suitcase in hand.[17]

Fhimah's diary, conveniently recovered and written in English (!), contained a reminder for 15 December to pick up Air Malta tags – a violation of airport and airline regulations. Al-Meghrahi, travelling under an alias, boarded LN 147 bound for Libya on the morning of 21 December 1988, overlapping the check-in time when the bomb was apparently inserted into the baggage of KM 180.

Al-Meghrahi's position and contacts in the Libyan intelligence apparatus placed him firmly in the camp of his first cousin Said Rashid – a leading architect and implementer of Libyan terrorist policies and a powerful member of the Libyan government's inner circle.[18] Rashid began direct attacks against US interests in late 1981, equipping Sudanese terrorists with decade timers in bombs containing Semtex-H. One such bomb, concealed in a cigarette carton, was used in a failed attempt to destroy a Pan Am flight in December 1983.[19]

In late 1985, 20 MST-13 timers manufactured exclusively by a Swiss electronics firm in Zurich, Meister et Bollier (MEBO), specifically for the Libyan External Security Organization were turned over to Said Rashid.[20] This was interesting because a circuit board fragment recovered from the Pan Am 103 bomb was part of a sophisticated timer which exactly resembled an electronic timer that Senegalese authorities discovered in the possession of two Libyan terrorists arrested in February 1988. Rashid also directed the bombing of La Belle disco in Berlin in April 1986, which is now known to have provoked the American bombing of Libya. However, in all this circumstantial evidence there was no direct link between Malta baggage and Pan Am 103.

The US Justice Department's suddenly blaming the two Libyans in 1991 triggered an outcry from the victims' families, who claimed that pointing the finger at Libya was a political ploy designed to reward Syria for siding with the US in the Gulf War and to help win the release of the hostages.[21] Subsequently, *Time* conducted a four-month investigation which produced fresh questions about the case against the Libyans. First, according to an FBI field report from Germany, the suitcase originating in Malta that supposedly contained the bomb may not have been transferred to Pan Am 103 in Frankfurt, as charged in the indictment of the two Libyans. Instead, the bomb-laden bag may have been substituted in Frankfurt for an innocent piece of luggage. Second, the rogue bag may have been placed on board the plane by Ahmed Jibril's group with the help of Monzer al-Kassar, a Syrian drug dealer who was co-operating with the US Drug Enforcement Agency. Thirdly, the report stated that Jibril and his group may have targeted that flight because an intelligence team led by Charles McKee of the Defence Intelligence Agency (DIA) was on board, whose job it was to find and rescue the hostages.[22] But as the *Time* report concluded, the US government's charges against al-Meghrahi and Fhimah do not explain how the bronze-coloured Samsonite suitcase, supposedly dispatched via Air Malta, eluded Frankfurt's elaborate airport security system. Months after the crash, FAG, the German company that operates the luggage transfer system, discovered the printout purportedly proving that the Libyans' suitcase sent from Malta was logged in at coding station 206 shortly after 1 pm. and then routed to Gate 44 in Terminal B, where it was put aboard Pan Am 103. But the FBI report neither indicated the origin of the bag that was sent for loading on Pan Am 103 nor that it was actually loaded on Pan Am 103. The FBI agent's report to the Director in Washington concludes, 'There remains the possibility that no luggage was transferred from Air Malta 180 to Pan Am 103.'[23] So, in 1991 different agencies of the US government still held opposite views about the responsibility for the bombing of Pan Am 103.

The Iranian Connection: Scenario I

A much more likely cause for the destruction of Pan Am 103 goes back to an incident in the Persian Gulf in July 1988. It has become widely accepted that the sequence of events leading to the Lockerbie incident began on 3 July 1988. While sailing in Iranian waters, the US Aegis-class cruiser *Vincennes* somehow mistook a commercial Iranian airbus that had just taken off from Bandar Abbas Airport for an Iranian F14 fighter closing in to attack, and shot it down. All 290 passengers on board were killed, most of them pilgrims on their way to Mecca.[24] The US government not only sought to excuse the blunder, but lied to Congress about it, lied in its official investigation of the incident, and handed out a Commendation Medal to the ship's air-warfare co-ordinator for his 'heroic achievement'.[25] The cruiser's commander, Captain Will Rogers III, still insists that the *Vincennes* was in international waters at the time and that he made the proper decision.

The Iranians were incensed. Paying the US Navy the compliment of believing that it knew what it was doing, they chose to construe America's evasive response to their complaint before the UN Security

Council as a cover-up for a deliberate act of aggression, rather than as an attempt to hide its embarrassment. To reaffirm the power of Islam and in retribution for the injury, the Ayatollah Khomeini himself is said to have ordered the destruction of not one, but four American flag carriers, although this was to be done discreetly.[26] His Minister of the Interior, Ali Akbar Mohtashemi. was placed in charge of planning Iran's revenge. At a meeting in Teheran on 9 July 1988, he awarded the contract to Ahmed Jibril's PFLP-GC.[27] Although Jibril later denied his complicity in the bombing, he was reported to have bragged among friends that the fee for the job was $10 million.

Jibril had specialized in aircraft bombings from 1970 onwards and his group was known for the sophistication of its explosive devices. Bombs designed to destroy an aircraft in flight often featured a barometric switch that could be used with or without a timer to detonate a charge at a predetermined altitude. Two such devices were seized by the Bundeskriminalamt (BKA), the German federal police, on 26 October 1988, eight weeks before Pan Am 103's fatal flight. Frankfurt was an important hub for US carriers, connecting with feeder airlines from all over Europe and the Middle East. Also with a sizeable Middle Eastern community living in Germany, Jibril knew he could count on the co-operation of local Islamic fundamentalists in Frankfurt, not least among them Turkish baggage handlers employed at the airport. Their skill in evading its security system had already proved most useful in promoting Syria's heroin exports.[28]

Jibril's senior lieutenant, Hafez Kassem Dalkamouni, was sent to Germany where, on 13 October, he was joined by the PFLP-GC's leading explosives expert and bombmaker, Marwan Abdel Khreesat, a Jordanian.[29] Acting on CIA and Mossad warnings, the BKA was watching these two men. By 25 October, four bombs in two Toshiba radio-cassette players, two hi-fi radio tuners and a video screen had been assembled. As Dalkamouni and Khreesat left the latter's apartment, carrying their luggage as if for the last time, they were arrested.[30] Operation Autumn Leaves, as the BKA called this exercise, only yielded one 312-gram Semtex-H bomb, moulded into the case of a black Toshiba radio cassette recorder, fitted with a barometric switch and time delay. It had been assembled for just one purpose – to destroy an aircraft in flight. An urgent warning was issued to airline security chiefs throughout the world to watch for Toshiba radios. In April 1989, two of the Khreesat bombs were found in Dalkamouni's brother-in-law's basement. This left one bomb unaccounted for.

Frankfurt Airport remained the best location from which to attack a US passenger aircraft, so Jibril reportedly turned for logistical support to Libya, the PFLP's principal supplier of Semtex-H. The mechanics of placing a bomb aboard an international flight were not difficult, but Jibril faced a serious conflict with the Syrian heroin cartel, based in Lebanon. Rifat Assad, brother of Syria's president Hafez Assad, and his associate Monzer al-Kassar between them controlled the flow of drugs along the pipeline from the Bekaa Valley to the US via Frankfurt and London.[31]

The Drug Smuggling Route – Scenario II

Al-Kassar was an arms dealer, armourer-in-chief to the PFLP-GC and other Palestinian extremist groups and also, through Lt. Col. Oliver North and former Air Force General Richard Secord, to the Contras in Nicaragua. He enjoyed protected status as a CIA asset and had intrigued his sponsors by acting as middleman in the ransom paid by the French government in 1986 to secure the release of two French hostages in Beirut.[32]

The CIA, under pressure from the Reagan White House, now sought al-Kassar's help in persuading the Syrian-backed terrorist factions in Lebanon to free American hostages. He said he would do what he could, but reminded them that he was also in the drug business and the CIA understood him perfectly.[33]

But Jibril also derived large funding from Syrian drug trafficking and realized that neither Rifat Assad, himself a CIA asset, nor al-Kassar would wish their drug pipeline through Frankfurt compromised by a terrorist attack which would show up the gaps in airport security. On the other hand, to refuse to co-operate would seem like a lack of zeal in the cause of Islam. Therefore, towards the end of October, Mossad observed Jibril and al-Kassar dining alone at a Lebanese restaurant in Paris, probably in an attempt to resolve the dilemma.[34] Neither man could afford to be entirely frank with the other, although in the end, al-Kassar must have promised to use his connections to get a bomb aboard an American flight from Frankfurt.

Besides the revolving door loyalties of al-Kassar and Assad, there was another variable in this equation called the Octopus Factor. With the CIA's permission, the US DEA in Cyprus played one target group off against another in an attempt to cripple both and so have some influence in the charnel house of Lebanese politics. For example, the Syrian presence was deeply resented by the well-armed and ferocious clans of the Bekaa Valley, which had previously run their family enclaves like independent principalities. So the DEA could only exploit their differences from a distance, in Cyprus, slowing down the export of narcotics, which had come to represent about 50 per cent of Lebanon's economic activity.[35]

To the CIA, the Assad - al-Kassar pipeline was both a bargaining chip for hostage retrieval and a vital link in its Middle East intelligence gathering network. To the US State Department, narcotics was virtually the sole means of economic support for the pro-Western Christian factions in Lebanon, without whom the whole country would collapse into the hands of the Shiite extremists. Narcotics law enforcement in Cyprus thus tended to proceed on the basis of *ad hoc* agreements between an assortment of government agents with different agendas, reflecting local priorities and for political reasons. It was aimed more at breaking up drug distribution rings in the US than at knocking out the Lebanese suppliers.

On 5 December 1988, the US Embassy in Helsinki received a telephone warning that within the next two weeks an attempt would be made to place a bomb aboard a Pan Am flight from Frankfurt to New York. On 8 December Israeli forces raided a PFLP-GC camp near Damour, Lebanon, and captured documents relating to a planned attack on a Pan Am flight out of Frankfurt later that month.[36] This information was passed on to the US and German governments.

At about the same time, and continuing until 20 December US intelligence monitoring the telephones of the Iranian Embassy in Beirut heard informant David Lovejoy brief the Iranian *chargé d'affaires* about the movements of a five-man CIA/DIA team, which had arrived in Lebanon to work at the release of US hostages and which planned to fly home from Frankfurt on Pan Am 103 on 21 December.[37]

The Hostage Recovery Team - Scenario III

In late December 1988, al-Kassar picked up some news that threatened to shut down his smuggling operation. Charles McKee's counter-terrorist team in Beirut had got wind of his CIA connection. The team was outraged that the COREA unit in Weisbaden was doing business with a Syrian with such close terrorist connections. After venting their anger to the CIA in Langley, Virginia, McKee and Matthew Gannon, the CIA's deputy chief of station in Beirut, on receiving no answer, decided to fly back to Virginia unannounced to expose the COREA unit's secret deal with al-Kassar. They packed $500,000 in cash, provided for the rescue mission of the hostages, and booked seats on Pan Am 103 out of London, connecting through Cyprus.[38] Apparently the team's movements were being tracked by the Iranians, since a story later appeared in the Arabic newspaper *Al-Dustura* of 22 May 1989, which disclosed that the terrorists set out to kill McKee and his team because of their planned hostage rescue attempt.

As the *Time* study pointed out, the theory that Jibril targetted Flight 103 in order to kill the hostage rescue team is supported by two independent intelligence experts. M. Gene Weaton, a retired US military intelligence officer with 17 years duty in the Middle East, sees chilling similarities between the Lockerbie crash and the suspicious DC-8 crash in Gander, Canada, which killed 248 American soldiers in 1985. Islamic Jihad actually boasted it had blown up the Arrow Air jet in phone calls in Oran, Algeria and to Reuters news agency in Beirut. In the latter, the caller stated that the Shiite Muslim extremist group planted a bomb on board to prove 'our ability to strike at the Americans anywhere'.[39]

Victor Marchetti, an intelligence writer and former executive assistant to the CIA's deputy director, believes that the team's presence on Flight 103 was like the loose thread of a sweater. 'Pull on it and the whole thing may unravel.' Marchetti believes the bombing of Flight 103 could have been avoided since 'the Mossad knew about it and didn't give proper warning and the CIA knew about it and screwed up'.[40]

On 18 December 1988, the BKA was tipped off about a bomb plot against Pan Am 103 in the next two or three days and this information was passed to the American Embassy in Bonn, which advised the State Department, which in turn advised its other embassies of the warning. On 20 December, Mossad passed on a similar warning, this time relating specifically to Flight 103 the next day.[41]

It is obvious that more than enough warning was given to many different agencies about the impending doom of Pan Am 103. One of these warnings may well have been telephoned by al-Kassar himself, knowing what kind of situation he had got himself into with Jibril.

Perhaps we will never know. As with Pearl Harbour, the information was in the system, but no one was co-coordinating it. Pan Am 103 raised the whole problem of what level of government warning should be issued and how public reported threats should be.[42] But in this case, too many government agencies were working at cross-purposes for an effective air security policy to be implemented. Contrary to US government policy officially condemning Libya, there seems to be overwhelming evidence that Pan Am 103 was an act of revenge on the part of the Iranians. The attack took place just four days before Christmas, and perhaps it is only a coincidence that the Iranian airbus was blown out of the sky four days before the feast day of Id al-Adha, the high point of the Muslim year.[43] If Pan Am 103 was destroyed because of Charles McKee and his team, then a long, critical look needs to be taken at US foreign policy. The same judgement is applicable if Pan Am 103 went down because of official tolerance of a drug trade that was being allowed to flourish by means of international public transport in order to save a doubtful ally in Lebanon.

Governments, Politics and Cover-ups

In 1992, James M. Shaughnessy, Pan Am's lead defence lawyer subpoenaed the FBI, CIA, DEA and four other government agencies for all documents pertaining to both the bombing of Flight 103 and the narcotics sting operation. Not surprisingly, he was repeatedly rebuffed by the Justice Department for reasons of national security. The stakes were enormous and the incentive high for Shaughnessy to demonstrate the government's responsibility for the bombing. He was bringing a claim against the government for failing to give warning that Pan Am had been targetted by the terrorists.[44]

As Rodney Wallis has written, prior to Lockerbie, at least three vital pieces of information were available to Pan American and US authorities:

> First, it was known that bombs intended for use against aircraft had been manufactured in West Germany. Second, a specific threat had been made against the airline. Third, the result of an ICAO study into the shooting down of an Iranian airbus by a U.S. warship had been published. The findings were unsatisfactory to Iran; they had wanted the United States to be condemned as aggressors.[45]

As Wallis further points out: 'Ever since the loss of the Iranian aircraft, civil aviation security experts had expected some retaliatory action to be taken against a United States target. The delay in a revenge attack was believed to hang on the ICAO study.'[46] When ICAO then failed to condemn the US, radicals within Iran could and did successfully demand direct action. This established a time scenario that was to dovetail into the Lockerbie tragedy. It also established motivation for an attack on a US aircraft.

In the USA, it was families and friends of the victims of Lockerbie who united into a powerful lobby group. They demanded and got a public, US-based investigation into the bombing. President Bush established a commission on Aviation, Security and Terrorism under the chair of a former labour secretary, Ann McLaughlin, announced on 4 August 1989. Concentrating on Pan Am 103, the commission's report was extremely critical of both the FAA and Pan American. It was recommended to the president that the US should prepare for 'pre-emptive or retaliatory strikes against known terrorist enclaves'.[47] As Wallis further points out, the key findings of the report were: 1. The US civil aviation security system was seriously flawed; 2. the FAA was a reactive agency; 3. Pan Am's apparent security lapses and the FAA's failure to enforce its own regulations followed a pattern that existed for months prior to Flight 103, during the tragedy and, notably, for nine months thereafter; 4. the destruction of Flight 103 may well have been preventable. Stricter baggage reconciliation procedures could have stopped any unaccompanied checked bags from boarding the flight at Frankfurt.[48]

What else could the government possibly say? Governments are not so stupid as to go out and perjure themselves. The responsibility for the destruction of Pan Am 103 and all its 270 victims and the 290 Iranian airbus victims lies squarely with the US government and the kind of foreign policy it chose to follow. US retaliation against Libya in 1986 was both undemocratic and provocative. It settled nothing and it did give Libya reason to continue its terrorism more stealthily and therefore more effectively. The shooting down of the Iranian airbus was either an act of international brigandage or it was a stupid mistake. Apologies could have been made and compensation paid. To leave the matter as it was, was bound to provoke Iran to take revenge in a devious and destructive way. And that's just what happened on 21 December 1988.

There were many warnings to the US government from the West

German BKA, from Mossad, from the phone call in Helsinki. There was clear evidence of a new terrorist phase developing in Western Europe. The government of the United States warned some of its personnel not to travel on Pan Am near Christmas. The public was left out of the warning and thus many innocent victims perished.

There was then the pathetic and lawless attempt by the US government to buy back American hostages by secretly giving arms to their sworn enemy Iran. The creation of a Restricted Inter-Agency Group in Washington led by Oliver North meant that one foreign policy (the NSC, the White House and the CIA) was in competition with another diametrically opposed foreign policy (Congress, the State Department, the Pentagon and public opinion).[49] One group wished to free the hostages, another was content to finance Lebanon's continuance by means of drug money.

Within the different agencies of the US government, the left hand didn't know what the right hand was doing. The CIA had its agenda, the DEA had its agenda and the DIA had yet another agenda. How, in these contradictory circumstances, could one possibly expect to develop effective civil aviation security?

The role of Monzer al-Kassar, the drug dealer, epitomizes the utter ambiguity of US policy. On one hand he was co-operating with the DEA and CIA and yet on the other hand he was related to the Syrian president by marriage and was co-operating with the Palestinian Jibril in destroying an American jumbo jet. On one hand the COREA (CIA) group out of Weisbaden was co-operating with al-Kassar in the drug trade and on the other a DIA group under McKee was planning to spring the hostages free. At the same time, a turncoat former CIA operative was advising the Iranian government how McKee and his group could be murdered. The American intelligence community was simply out of control.

It is certainly true that a public warning to all airlines and passengers as well as passenger baggage reconciliation could have been implemented. They might have prevented Pan Am 103, but an act of government is necessary to tighten security and put airlines on the alert and the American government simply failed to do this in the face of overwhelming indications of danger. No government, of course, is perfect and mistakes will be made, but the Pan Am 103 fiasco shows that when the different agencies of government are pulling in different directions and jurisdictional non-communication is the general rule, you have a disaster in the making.

In an article in *The Listener*, on 8 January 1987, appropriately entitled 'Democracy must not be held to ransom by terrorism', Professor Paul Wilkinson states, 'It is my profound belief that these fundamental policy issues [about terrorism] can and must be properly debated by a democratic society. The evolution of anti-terrorist policy should not be the monopoly of experts ... In a democratic system no long-term policy will survive unless it is sustained by a high degree of popular support.'

Wilkinson goes on to suggest that

> when policy on terrorism is left to a small, self-appointed elite, the danger is that you get incompetent and foolish men conducting bad policy and that they get away with it because they have deliberately evaded public and legislative scrutiny and accountability. The Irangate scandal, the Reagan administration's arms for hostages deal with Iran and the diversion of some of the profits to the Contras provides a dreadful warning of the dangers and corrupting effects of abuse of secret power.[50]

The message of this case study is that aircraft security is at the mercy of erratic foreign policy.

Conclusions

The case study of Pan Am 103 has been used to illustrate the intensely political nature of aviation terrorism. It has sought to demonstrate that two highly-volatile political movements (the Palestinians and Iranian-driven Islamic fundamentalism) joining forces and pooling resources could and did cause extraordinary confusion and damage to international civil aviation. The unresolved problem of the Palestinians drove radical rejectionist groups throughout the 1970s and 1980s to attack civil aviation, especially but not exclusively in Western Europe. During the 1980s, various Islamic fundamentalist groups began hijacking, and then sabotaging civil aircraft. These two political forces then came together in the Pan Am 103 bombing.

In an article detailing the upswing of terrorist attacks in and against the United States in *The Washington Quarterly* in early 1998, David Tucker, who works in the office of the assistant secretary of defence for special operations and low-intensity conflict, listed nine ways the US has combated terrorism over the years. It has negotiated international legal conventions, implemented defensive measures, followed a policy of no concessions, imposed economic sanctions, retaliated militarily, pre-empted terrorist attacks, disrupted terrorist organizations, prosecuted suspected terrorists and addressed the causes of terrorism. Today, a policy of no concessions, prosecution and economic sanctions remain the principal weapons employed against terrorism.[51]

It is remarkable that little attention is now paid to understanding and addressing the causes of terrorism. On the tenth anniversary of the Pan Am 103 disaster, it seems an optimum time to recognize that terrorism is not just about law and order, but about politics and social justice. Thus, when considering the twin problems of the Palestinians and Islamic fundamentalism, we need to recognize that we are dealing with a global structural problem, which has become solidly internationalized. By internationalized, we mean that it has become a matter of profound concern to the international community, a concern not yet shared by the USA because of its blind commitment to Israel, right or wrong, and its black and white attitudes toward change in Iran and the Middle East.

Like huge boils on the international body politic, these basic problems need to be lanced and drawn out. Poultices and bandages will not do any longer, because these problems have transcended national and regional levels. They have become what one might describe as international regimes of terrorist violence. Fundamentalists and Palestinians alike are calling for collective action to bring about social and political change. Hijacking is one of the sticks used to beat recalcitrants into action.

The policies of the West and Israel have led to severe dispersal and acute statelessness for the Palestinians, who are resourceful and highly-educated people. Because of the length of their suffering, they have created communities within Western cities, which could easily become staging posts of future conflict. By the same token, Islamic fundamentalism is presenting itself as a radical Islamic alternative to the tired, secular authoritarian regimes of the Middle East that are perceived to have sold out to the West.

In the 1990s, fundamentalist terrorism has launched major attacks on the USA, both within and outside the country. Unless the problems raised here are addressed, much worse could be in store for the USA in the future. The final conclusion of this analysis is therefore that a new level of Western co-operation is called for, not just to tighten air security, but to exercise a common political will to solve the grievances at the heart of the Palestinian and Islamic fundamentalist movements. Putting it another way, the unhappy progression of thirty years of hijacking has been largely caused by the failure of governments to deal with the Middle Eastern turmoil.

NOTES

1. Cited in O.P. St. John, *Air Piracy, Airport Security & International Terrorism* (Westport, CT: Quorum Books, 1991), pp.109–10.
2. Ibid,. p.68.
3. Ibid.
4. The correct term for hijacking is 'unlawful interference', but it is not a term that is easily understood, hence my use of 'hijack'.
5. Claude Bergeron, 'Unlawful Interference with Civil Aviation: 1968–88', in David Charters (ed.), *Democratic Responses to International Terrorism* (New York: Transnational Publishers, 1991), p.38.
6. Peter St. John, 'Counterterrorism Policy-Making: The Case of Aircraft Hijacking: 1968–88' in ibid., p.69.
7. Ibid, pp.73–4.
8. Ibid, pp.108–09.
9. Bergeron in Charters (note 5), p.58.
10. Rodney Wallis, *Combating Air Terrorism* (London: Brassey's, 1991).
11. Internationalization of a domestic political problem means that the problem has become the concern of and is likely to be at least partly mediated by the international community.
12. Wallis (note 10), p.26.
13. St..John (note 1), p.21.
14. Bergeron in Charters (note 5), p.50.
15. St John (note 1), pp.153–9.
16. David Leppard, *On the Trail of Terror,* (London 1991, p.27.
17. Ibid., p.22.
18. G. Simons, *Libya: The Struggle for Survival* (New York 1993), p.88.
19. Ibid., p.61.
20. Ibid., p.54.
21. *Time,* 27 April 1992. p.23.
22. Ibid., pp.22–3.
23. Ibid., pp.32.
24. M. Cox and T. Foster, *Their Darkest Day* (New York 1992), p.98.
25. David Johnson, *Lockerbie,* (London: Bloomsbury, 1989), p.21.
26. Cox and Foster (note 24), p.38.
27. Sanya Popovic, in the *Globe and Mail,* Toronto, 27 Nov. 1993. p.A17.
28. *Time,* (note 21), p.26.
29. D. Goddard and L.K. Coleman, *Trail of the Octopus,* (London 1993), p.14.
30. Ibid., p.15.
31. Goddard and Coleman (note 29), p.17.
32. Cox and Foster (note 24), p.47.
33. S. Emmerson and B. Duffy, *The Fall of Pan Am 103,* (London 1990), p.6. See also *Time* (note 21), pp.27–8.
34. *Time* (note 21), p.27.

35. Ibid., p.30.
36. Ibid., p.28.
37. Goddard and Coleman (note 29), p. 19.
38. Ibid., p.27.
39. Ibid., p.30.
40. Ibid., p.28.
41. Goddard and Coleman (note 29), p.19.
42. See the discussion of this important matter in Wallis (note 10), p.122.
43. Goddard and Coleman (note 29), p.20.
44. *Time* (note 21), p.26.
45. Wallis (note 10), p.27.
46. Ibid., p.28.
47. Ibid., p.33.
48. Ibid., p.50.
49. See Bob Woodward, *Veil: The Secret Wars of the CIA 1981–87* (New York: Pocket Books, 1987).
50. Paul Wilkinson, 'Democracy must not be held to ransom by terrorism', in *The Listener,* 8 Jan. 1987, p.4.
51. David Tucker, 'Responding to Terrorism', in *The Washington Quarterly,* Winter 1998, p.104.

4

Aircraft Sabotage

BRIAN M. JENKINS

One of the deadliest threats posed by contemporary terrorists is the sabotage of passenger aircraft. Since 1969, there have been more than 70 known attempts to plant bombs on board airliners. These have caused at least 15 crashes, killing 1,732 persons. There are several more crashes where sabotage is strongly suspected but not confirmed. And there may be foiled plots and near misses that we know nothing about. These incidents conform to a disturbing terrorist trend toward large-scale indiscriminate violence. Truck bombs – massive quantities of crude explosives on wheels, and sabotage of aircraft – small sophisticated bombs designed to elude detection by security systems, account for the bloodiest terrorist incidents: the 1985 sabotage of an Air India flight (329 dead), the 1993 car bombing in Bombay's financial district (more than 300 killed), the 1988 sabotage of Pan Am 103 (270 dead), the 1983 truck bomb attack on the US Marine barracks in Beirut (241 dead), the 1989 sabotage of a French UTA airliner (171 dead), the 1995 Oklahoma City bombing (168 dead), and the 1987 sabotage of a Korean airliner (115 dead).

The incidents also conform to a terrorist tendency to target public transportation that offers terrorists concentrations of people – mostly strangers – in enclosed environments, and generally poses little security challenge and allows easy escape. In addition to attacks on airlines, terrorists, in recent years, have detonated bombs aboard buses in Israel, the Paris Metro, trolleys in Moscow, and dispersed nerve gas in Tokyo's subways. Indeed, there is some concern that as aviation security improves, terrorists will increasingly attack surface transportation systems, which are much more difficult to protect.

Few of the airline crashes are credibly claimed by any terrorist group, although, of course, there are always claims by someone, even for crashes where no sabotage is involved; usually these are easily dismissed as hoaxes. The absence of terrorist claims for true acts of sabotage puzzles those accustomed to thinking that all terrorist actions must be claimed in order to have potential meaning. This is not the case. In fact only about half of all incidents of international terrorism are credibly claimed. In another quarter of the incidents, the likely perpetrators are easily identified, but the remaining quarter requires sleuthing.

The lack of claims may reflect the changing motives and organisational patterns of terrorism. When terrorists pursued political goals on behalf of identifiable, if imaginary, constituencies, a claim of responsibility was seen as contributing to the achievement of the terrorists' objectives. Terrorists working on behalf of state sponsors, determined solely to punish their perceived enemies, or inspired by religious fanaticism with God or His self-appointed spokesperson as their sole constituent, have no need to claim responsibility. Unclaimed attacks may also simply be more terrifying, as they give us no enemy to identify. The absence of a claim seems to correspond with the scale of death. Five of the seven deadliest terrorist incidents listed above went unclaimed. Of the 15 airline crashes caused by bombs, terrorists claimed responsibility for only six of them.

The Popular Front for the Liberation of Palestine-General Command (PFLP–GC), which introduced the altitude-detonated bomb, claimed responsibility for the 1970 crash of a Swiss flight to Tel Aviv, which killed 47 people. Croatian separatists claimed responsibility for the 1971 crash of a Stockholm-to-Belgrade airline that crashed, killing 26. Although another Arab group claimed responsibility for the 1974 crash of a TWA airliner flying from Athens to Tel Aviv, which killed 88 persons, investigators later determined that the bomb had been planted by the PFLP–GC. Sikh separatists calling themselves the Dashmesh Regiment claimed responsibility for the 1985 crash of an Air India flight, and the 'Extraditables', Colombian terrorists backed by drug traffickers, claimed responsibility for the crash of an Avianca jetliner in 1989. A Lebanon-based group using the name Partisans of God claimed responsibility for the crash of a Panamanian commuter plane in 1994.

Including all attempts to sabotage aircraft shows the perpetrators to be a diverse lot that includes criminal extortionists; Eritrean, Croatian and Sikh separatists; Colombian drug lords; anti-Castro Cubans; Palestinians; Shi'ite fanatics; agents of Iran, Iraq, Libya, Syria, and North Korea. Middle Eastern groups collectively account for more than half of the known attempts. They have built the most sophisticated devices and have been the most successful. They are believed responsible for two-thirds of the cases where bombs brought planes down or at least exploded while the plane was in the air.

Terrorists want to ensure that their bombs go off while the plane is in flight. Most bombs also were intended to detonate while the plane was over the water thus making evidence difficult to recover. Terrorists initially relied on timing devices, but timing devices alone proved unreliable since flight delays may result in the bomb going off while the plane is still on the ground. Altimeter-detonated bombs worked better but meant the bomb would go off on the next leg of the flight. By the late 1980s, terrorists had developed a combination timer and altimeter detonation system to provide greater control over when the explosion would occur.

How successful were they? In 24 of the known attempts, terrorists succeeded in detonating a bomb on board while the plane was in the air; 15 planes went down but nine of the damaged aircraft still managed to land safely. In 13 more cases, delays saved lives as the bombs detonated before departure. In the remaining cases, the bomb failed to detonate or was discovered and disarmed. There are no known cases where terrorists successfully carried out sabotage in the traditional manner; that is, by causing mechanical failure without the use of explosives.

Some of the past bombings have been part of a campaign or 'barrage' of aircraft bombings. The Eritrean Liberation Front planted bombs aboard Ethiopian Airlines jets in March 1969 and again a year later. Firebombs were planted aboard four Iberian Airlines flights on the same day in May 1970. Anti-Castro extremists planted bombs aboard airliners in November 1975 and again in October 1976. Palestinian terrorists planted bombs aboard two Pan Am flights in August 1982. Sikh separatists tried to bring down three flights in June 1985. There were attempts to smuggle bombs on to El Al flights in April and June 1986. The most ambitious scheme was that of the Islamic militant Ramzi Yousef, who plotted to blow up 12 US airliners in the Pacific region in 1995.

How were the bombs smuggled on board? In more than two-thirds of the cases where we have adequate information, the bombs were hidden in checked luggage, sent as mail, or placed in the cargo. In another quarter of the cases, bombs were carried on board in hand luggage, then concealed in the lavatories (the most popular hiding spot in the passenger compartment), or under the seats. In several cases, terrorists bombers hid the bomb in the cockpit and, in one case, in the landing gear well (where illegal aliens have sometimes attempted to hide).

As security measures increased over the years, bombs were skillfully disguised to appear as other objects – tape cassette players or as part of the suitcase itself. Terrorists put bombs in bags, then missed their flights. (Ensuring that there is a passenger on board for each checked piece of luggage prevents this.) Or they carried bombs on board, concealed them in the cabin, then left the aircraft at the next stop. Very few terrorists have been willing to carry out suicide missions; in other cases, unwitting passengers were duped into carrying bombs on board, which is why travellers are now asked if anyone has given them any gifts or asked them to carry parcels. In at least one case, an official at the airport was coerced into planting a bomb on a plane by terrorists who threatened to kill his family if he did not co-operate.

Shoulder-fired, heat-seeking, surface-to-air missiles have become more available to guerrillas and terrorists in recent years, and have been used to bring down civilian airliners in Africa and Asia. Thus far, we have not seen their use outside of conflict zones, but it remains a potential future scenario.

The persistent problems in screening luggage and cargo, inspecting planes before they are turned around to fly, protecting aircraft against unauthorised access, and maintaining the efficiency and fidelity of employees remain the principal vulnerabilities.

5

Aviation Security and Terrorism:
An Analysis of the Potential Threat
to Air Cargo Integrators

BRUCE HOFFMAN

In recent years, regulations have been proposed both in Europe and the United States that would apply identical security procedures to pure cargo as well as to passenger aircraft. The assumption behind this policy change is that the threat posed by terrorists to commercial aviation is equal to both categories of air carrier. Its underlying reasoning was alluded to at a 1992 meeting held at Berne of the 'Sub Group for the Study of Operational Aspects of Security Problems', when essentially anecdotal evidence was offered as sufficient explanation for so considerable a policy change. The report of the Task Force on Cargo Security, for example, had only the following to say about so profound a proposed change to the existing regulations:

> While it was observed that the threat to freighter aircraft might be less than to a passenger aircraft and the consequences of a successful attack on a freighter aircraft less costly in terms of human life, it was difficult to be sure onto which type of aircraft a piece of cargo would be carried ... [Accordingly it] was agreed that cargo security measures should apply to both passenger and to freighter aircraft.[1]

This article assesses the validity and relevance of that rationale specifically as it applies to air cargo integrators: that is, commercial cargo shipping concerns whose primary business is the guaranteed, expeditious (often overnight) international delivery of letters, documents and small parcels (e.g., such well-known corporate entities as FedEx, UPS, and TNT among others).

The Terrorist Threat to Civil Aviation: An Overview[2]

Terrorism and commercial aviation share a common history.[3] Indeed, the advent of what is considered modern, contemporary, international terrorism began with a terrorist act involving a commercial passenger aircraft. On 22 July 1968, three armed Palestinian terrorists hijacked an Israeli El Al commercial flight en route from Rome to Tel Aviv. Although commercial aircraft had been hijacked before – this was the twelfth such incident in 1968 alone – the El Al hijacking differed significantly from all previous ones.

First, its purpose was not simply the diversion of a scheduled flight from one destination to another, as had been the case since 1959 when a seemingly endless succession of homesick Cubans or sympathetic revolutionaries from other countries had commandeered domestic American passenger aircraft simply as a means to travel to Cuba. This hijacking was a bold political statement. The three terrorists who seized the El Al flight had done so with the express purpose of trading the passengers they held hostage for Palestinian terrorists imprisoned in Israel.

Second, unlike previous hijackings, where the choice or nationality of the aircraft that was being seized did not matter (as long as the plane itself was capable of transporting the hijacker(s) to a desired destination), El Al – as Israel's national airline and by extension, therefore, a readily evident national 'symbol' of the Israeli state – had been specifically and deliberately targeted by the terrorists.

Finally, by taking control of an already controlled environment – where no entry or exit was possible while the aircraft was inflight and particularly where the movement and the behaviour of a relatively large number of passengers could be closely monitored by a handful of persons while the consequences of a government ignoring or rejecting the terrorists' demands could potentially be catastrophic (i.e., causing the destruction of the aircraft and deaths of all persons on board) – terrorists throughout the world discovered that they had essentially created a travelling 'theatre'. The intense media coverage that attended such events, could be used by the terrorists to attract, focus and keep the world's attention on the plight of the aircraft and its hapless passengers for a prolonged period of time.

The four basic characteristics of the El Al hijacking – the air carrier as political 'symbol', encapsulating the terrorists' animus against a specified 'enemy state'; the act as a 'political statement' designed to have repercussions beyond the aircraft itself and the passengers (i.e., victims) on board and thereby reach a wider 'target audience'; the air carrier as a 'national symbol' of the terrorists' enemy state – whether a designated official, 'national carrier' or because of its popular association in the public mind with a particular country or destination – identical to its embassies, consulates or other symbols of national sovereignty; and, its 'theatrical' dimension as an assured means, given the innocent civilian passengers on board, for terrorists to dramatically and incontrovertibly attract attention to themselves and their cause, continue today to influence terrorist decision-making and targeting regarding commercial aviation. Indeed, we will return to these four fundamental characteristics later in assessing the terrorist threat specifically to air cargo integrators.

At the time, the success of the hijacking sent a powerful message to terrorists everywhere. For both tactical and strategic reasons, commercial aviation was viewed as an attractive and potentially lucrative target. The comparative ease with which a plane could be seized, the confined space which could be readily controlled, the seated hostages who could be easily intimidated and managed, and the inherent drama and media attention which a hijacked plane-load of innocent civilians carried with it, were evident to terrorists and others who, during the succeeding 17 months, carried out an additional 89 acts of air piracy, bringing the number of airline hijackings between 1968 and 1969 to a total of 100.[4]

The installation of metal detectors (magnetometers) and attendant pre-boarding inspection of passengers and their carry-on items that became standard after 1973 have played a critical role in reducing the number of hijacks.[5] Only nine hijackings occurred in 1973, for example, compared to 30 in 1972. The annual number of hijackings similarly declined from an average 50 per year for 1968–69 to 18 per year for both the 1970s and 1980s, before decreasing still further during the first half of the 1990s to the lowest level since 1968: an average of only 14.4 per year.[6] The effect of the decrease in hijackings achieved between 1969 to 1979, for example, is shown in the results of a 1979 study, which concluded that the likelihood of a commercial aviation passenger being hijacked in the United States had dropped from 3.5 chances in 100,000 before the installation of metal detectors in 1973 to just 1 in 100,000 afterwards.[7] Additional security measures that have been enacted since that time, such as 'profiling' of passengers at check-in by specially trained security personnel – which El Al pioneered and since 1986 has been adopted by other 'high risk' national carriers such as those of United States airlines – largely account for the vast reduction in airline hijackings achieved thus far during the 1990s.

Viewed from another perspective, during the late 1960s, hijacking of passenger aircraft was among terrorists' favoured tactics, accounting for 33 per cent of all terrorist incidents worldwide. However, as security at airports improved, the incidence of airline hijackings declined to just seven percent of all international terrorist incidents in the 1970s and only four percent for both the 1980s and for the first half of the 1990s. But while these measures were successful in reducing airline hijackings, they did not stop terrorist attacks on commercial airlines altogether. Instead, prevented from smuggling weapons on board to hijack aircraft, terrorists merely continued to attack commercial aviation by means of bombs hidden in carry-on or checked baggage.

It should first be emphasised that despite media impressions to the contrary, terrorist bombings or even attempted bombings of aircraft while inflight are comparatively rare. They amounted to only 15 incidents between 1970 and 1979 (out of a total of 2,537 international terrorist incidents – or 0.6 per cent), and just 12 between 1980 and 1989 (out of a total of 3,943 international terrorist incidents – or an even lower 0.3 per cent of incidents). Indeed, this trend has continued throughout the first half of the current decade. There have been a total of just six inflight bombings since 1990 compared with a total of 1,859 international terrorist incidents thus far this decade. In other words, inflight bombings of commercial aviation account for 0.3 per cent of international terrorist attacks during the 1990s.[8] Nonetheless, the dramatic loss of life and attendant intense media coverage have turned those few events into terrorist 'spectaculars': etched indelibly on the psyches of commercial air travellers and security officers everywhere despite the extreme infrequency or likelihood of their occurrence, especially when compared to the millions of commercial flights that are completed safely on a daily basis at airports throughout the world.[9]

The overall paucity of inflight bombings is attributable in part to successful passenger baggage reconciliation practices (i.e., where a positive match is effected before take-off between all baggage in the cargo hold with every passenger). Since these practices were instituted following the inflight bombing of an Air India flight in 1985, in which all 328 persons on board had perished, a total of some 14 billion pieces of baggage have been screened and matched, with only three bombs[10] (with admittedly tragic results) having failed to be detected.[11] These 'first generation' measures, moreover, have been further strengthened as a result of the new security measures undertaken in the wake of the 1988 Pan Am 103 bombing.

In sum, therefore, one can conclude beyond any doubt that the incidence of terrorist bombings of passenger aircraft has declined appreciably over the past three decades. Moreover, when viewed from the wider perspective of overall worldwide trends in international terrorist activity, both in statistical and actual terms, the terrorist threat to commercial aviation cannot be judged as a salient, much less significantly active, trend of international terrorism today.

Patterns of Terrorist Operations and Tactics

In the above context, it is important to note that, generally speaking, overall terrorist operations and tactics reveal a remarkably low degree of innovation in contrast to a very high degree of imitation. This has significant implications for terrorist targeting of commercial aviation, and, in fact, explains the comparative paucity of terrorist bombing of aircraft. Terrorists are first and foremost 'success' freaks. That is, they arguably have a higher institutional imperative to succeed than any other type of organisation or group. Simply put, the terrorist act has to succeed if the terrorists are indeed to 'terrorise' anyone; i.e., put pressure on governments to act in a manner advantageous to the terrorists or generally create a climate of fear and intimidation amenable to terrorist exploitation. For this reason, terrorists have historically been remarkably risk-averse, adhering to the same narrow, 'tried and true' repertoire of tactics. As terrorists want to ensure that their operations have the highest likelihood or margin of success, the vast majority of their attacks are therefore not tactically innovative. Thus it can be said that, radical though their politics may be, they are commensurably conservative in their operations, rarely deviating from the familiar and adhering to an established *modus operandi* that, in their minds at least, minimises failure and maximises success.

Terrorists, therefore, seem to prefer the assurance of modest success to more complicated and complex operations which may have potentially higher pay-off in terms of casualties and publicity. Indeed, this explanation possibly accounts for the overall paucity of terrorist 'spectaculars' and the mostly limited number of casualties historically inflicted in terrorist attacks (i.e., more often in the tens and twenties and only occasionally ever stretching into the low hundreds). Indeed, since the beginning of the century fewer than a dozen terrorist incidents have occurred that resulted in the deaths of more than a 100 persons at one time.[12]

This identifiable trend has several implications for terrorist targeting of aircraft. First, it suggests a reluctance to undertake operations that do not have a large, virtually assured, margin of success. For example, if terrorists are inherently 'success freaks', they must also be 'control freaks' in order to 'influence' and affect the environment in which their operation takes place as a means of ensuring its 'successful' outcome. The obvious uncertainties of the commercial aviation environment created by the succession of security measures that have been continually adopted over the years may explain why terrorists in fact so infrequently target aircraft.[13] An operation against a commercial aircraft can be upset not only through the discovery of the explosive device through baggage screening or passenger profiling, but through unanticipated delays in departure, mis-routed baggage or even a malfunctioning bomb.[14] In 1985, for example, a bomb exploded at Japan's Narita Airport, killing two workers and wounding four others, while baggage was being unloaded from a Canadian Pacific Airlines flight. Doubtless this bomb was intended – like the one later that same day on a Montreal to London Air India flight which then crashed into the Irish Sea – to explode whilst the plane was inflight over water, thus rendering forensic investigation far more difficult, if not impossible. Moreover, even successful bombings may not go according to plan: Pan Am 103 is perhaps the archetypal example, as the explosion was meant to occur (like the 1985 Air India inflight bombing) while the aircraft was over water in order similarly to thwart investigation.

Accordingly, what innovation does occur in terrorist operations both in general as well as specifically directed against commercial aviation, is mostly in the methods used to conceal and detonate explosive devices not in the type of target or even in the actual tactics themselves.[15] In this respect, terrorists mostly seek to imitate previously successful attacks against identical target sets using the same tactics (whether by other terrorists or non-political criminals) rather than experiment with either new tactics or against different types of targets (i.e., air cargo integrators or air cargo carriers rather than commercial passenger aircraft). This proclivity towards imitation rather than innovation is arguably most clearly evidenced by the history of inflight bombing of passenger aircraft itself.

We forget that this tactic is by no means a new phenomenon. Indeed, the first recorded incident of an inflight bombing of a commercial passenger aircraft occurred more than 60 years ago when a bomb exploded on a United Airlines transcontinental passenger flight over Chesterton, Indiana, on 10 October 1933, killing all seven persons on board. Although no motive or suspects were ever uncovered, this was most probably *not* a politically-motivated attack (i.e., terrorism) but one executed for criminal (i.e., insurance fraud) or highly personal, idiosyncratic (i.e., psychological instability) motives. Not until 1949, when a Filipino woman and her lover hired two ex-convicts to place a bomb on a Philippines Airline flight, is there any evidence of a similar type of incident occurring. The motive was clearly criminal: the bomb was meant to kill the woman's husband, a passenger on the flight, in order to collect his inheritance and enable the woman to marry her lover. The bomb exploded killing all 13 persons on board. Just four months later another spouse, this time a Canadian male, placed a time bomb on a Canadian Pacific Airlines flight similarly in hopes of killing his wife, a passenger on the flight, and thereby collecting on her insurance policy. The device, which was concealed in the unfortunate woman's luggage, exploded in the forward baggage compartment whilst the plane was some 40 miles from Quebec City, killing all the aircraft's 23 passengers and crew. It is widely presumed that the bomber had read about the recent Philippines incident. Six years later, on 1 November 1955, in still another insurance collection plot, a son killed his mother and 44 other passengers on a United Airlines DC-6B jet, using a dynamite bomb that had been placed in her suitcase and checked in the luggage hold.[16]

The point, with regard to all the above incidents, is that long before terrorists began to attack passenger aircraft with bombs, assorted criminals, frustrated lovers and plain lunatics were 'pioneering' the use of such tactics against the same targets.[17] Accordingly, one can persuasively argue that terrorists only later adapted a tactic that had already proven its success. The implications of this 'copycat' factor of terrorism with regard to air cargo integrators is clear: terrorists themselves rarely innovate, relying instead on proven tactics against previously tried targets utilising techniques of the past. Accordingly, as no adversarial terrorist action has ever occurred (at least that we are aware of) against an air cargo integrator, this particular target of commercial aviation has arguably not attracted terrorist attention. In this context, moreover, it should be emphasised that there is no conclusive evidence that terrorists have ever attempted to place a bomb among the cargo carried by integrators, much less in the air cargo processed by commercial passenger airlines.

Moreover, within the context of air cargo integrators, this element of assured 'success' (that is, of terrorists thereby having complete 'control' over an operation is critical to understanding why this particular target set, i.e., air cargo integrators) would not only be unattractive to terrorists but might perhaps also serve as a formidable deterrent. Two key elements of air cargo integrator operations virtually deprive terrorists of the predictability and certainty of timing that they crave. One is the integrators' inherent multi-modal distribution system the other is the uniquely specialised service that the integrators provide based on the most expeditious delivery possible of a consignment. Indeed, the *raison d'être* for the integrator's very existence – speed of delivery – requires an exploitation of all available ground transport resources[18] that renders impossible predictability and certainty of a specific carrier, much less its flight, time of departure, planned route, and so on. Accordingly, terrorists cannot ascertain, much less predict, the exact time that a particular item will be in transit, except to assume that it will likely be transported between point A and point B as expeditiously as possible, or even from which airport or to what intermediate destination it might depart and over what route it will travel. This lack of control, therefore, severely militates against any exact planning or timing. Surely, this uncertainty and 'unscheduled' dimension of the movement of air integrator cargo alone must seriously negate any terrorist attempt to exploit this means of transport.

Moreover, the strict accounting measures and 'paper trail' requirements both to manage the expeditious delivery process and for efficacious Customs clearance procedures still further diminishes the terrorist threat. Since every item accepted for transit is meticulously logged and accounted for on a computerised database, with exact details of the sending and receiving parties, date and time of pick-up, originating location, delivery location and so on meticulously recorded, the forensic evidence that would be available to law enforcement authorities in the event that terrorists might attempt to exploit this avenue of supposed attack becomes extremely daunting. By contrast, for example, passengers on commercial flights regularly arrive at airport check-ins with no readily available or accurate means of verifying from where specifically their journey originated or where specifically they are going once they depart the aircraft at their destination. The only information required is a ticket and a passport. On the other hand, because of the nature of the service they provide, air integrators must routinely record on secure automated systems all details for each consignment in order to track with the greatest degree of accuracy all items' movement from pick-up to delivery. As one analysis concluded, 'forwarders usually know more about a shipment than the carriers'.[19]

Obviously, this tracking requirement is particularly critical in facilitating Customs clearance, thus further enhancing consignment accountability. Equally obviously, Customs' concerns with narcotics trafficking via parcels consigned to air cargo integrators, or the illicit movement of cash across international borders, imposes a high degree of standardisation of practice, which readily identifies suspicious anomalies and in turn suspect parcels or letters. Moreover, in order to facilitate the expeditious movement and delivery of items, Customs themselves have direct access to air integrator computer systems. The argument raised by the European Express Organisation itself is surely pertinent to this argument: 'The discovery risks inherent in exposing themselves to such systems are well understood by many who have fallen foul of them and there is no reason to believe that they are not equally well known in the world of the terrorist'.[20] Indeed, the aforementioned terrorist operational imperative to succeed clearly suggests that terrorists would avoid so stringent and standardised control procedures and so daunting a routinised audit trail is of itself a significant deterrent to terrorists as well.

Why Terrorists Target Aircraft

Although terrorists are often portrayed by the media or assumed in the public mind to be random and indiscriminate, if not irrational, this is not true. Terrorists select targets with high 'symbolic' value. For this reason, as noted previously, national air carriers have been attractive targets for terrorists as a means to strike at a less well-protected symbol of a hated enemy than, for example, an embassy or a consulate. Almost without exception, therefore, the 67 identified terrorist bombings of commercial aircraft that have occurred since 1968 *all* targeted recognised national carriers, not the far less well-known dedicated air cargo carriers, much less the arguably slightly better known charter passenger aircraft. Hence, in all these terrorist incidents involving commercial passenger carriers, the terrorists' intent was to strike directly at a symbol of national sovereignty. For this reason, terrorists target *specific* symbols of a nation-state as embodied in a state's national passenger air carriers. Obviously, recognised 'national' carriers (whether state-owned or privatised), such as Israel's El Al Airlines, France's Air France, the United Kingdom's British Airways or India's Air India, will lead the list of attractive targets; while other carriers known more perhaps for their association with a particular country, such as Canadian Airlines (formerly Candian Pacific), Pan Am, United, American, Delta, and so on, that are widely known as Canadian or United States-based airlines flying on Canadian or United States routes, will also attract terrorist interest because of their 'symbolic' value.

It is unclear, if not extremely doubtful, whether an attack on an air cargo integrator that is known, if at all, to the general public through an 'alphabet soup' of letters or innocuous corporate names such as TNT, UPS, FedEx, and so on, which are completely divorced from any identifiable national affiliation, would generate the same intense concern as an attack against a more familiar 'name-brand' passenger carrier. This argument alone renders any divining or hypothesis of a terrorist motive in targeting an air cargo integrator difficult, if not impossible.

To sum up then, in no way can one argue that air cargo integrators such as FedEx, UPS, and TNT have anywhere near the same nationalist associations or symbolic connotations and, most importantly, name recognition, of such well-known national carriers as El Al, British Airways, or Air France, or the obvious country associations of United, American Airlines, Delta, and so on, who are popularly linked to the United States and these other countries because of advertising, routes, and so on. Moreover, since many of the air cargo integrators have a worldwide commercial remit, rather than the direct geographical route associations of most 'national' passenger air carriers, it is doubtful that terrorists could reap any advantages from attacking them as opposed to those of the arguably far more publicity-rich commercial air carriers.

The 1990–91 Gulf War Exemplar

It has been suggested that terrorists supposedly intent on paralysing worldwide air traffic might resort to placing bombs indiscriminately in consignments transported by air cargo integrator parcels in order to achieve this end. To date, however, even at times of *extreme* international crisis or tension, such as the 1990–91 Gulf War when this threat might have been anticipated, it never in fact materialised. Indeed, given that so much terrorist activity, as noted above, is imitative and not innovative, the previous absence of any plot of this type in cases of extreme international tension arguably vitiates this possibility at all other times.

For example, almost from the start of the conflict in August 1990, when Iraq invaded Kuwait and US forces were deployed to defend Saudi Arabia against Iraqi aggression, thinly-veiled threats began to emanate from the Middle East warning of terrorist actions in response to the American and coalition forces' intervention. Saddam Hussein called on fellow Muslims to embark on a holy war against the United States and attack American interests wherever they could be reached.[21] Abul Abbas, the Palestinian terrorist who masterminded the 1985 hijacking of the Italian cruise ship, *Achille Lauro,* ordered his men to 'Open fire on the American enemy everywhere'.[22] Not to be outdone by a rival's clarion call to battle, Abu Nidal, the architect of the brutal machine gun and hand grenade attacks on the Rome and Vienna airports in 1985, immediately followed suit, warning that his organisation was preparing to carry out '90 attacks in 20 countries' against US and Western targets. George Habash, the founder and leader of the Popular Front for the Liberation of Palestine, went a step further, threatening American cities with nuclear terrorist attacks.

Throughout the long build-up of US and coalition forces in the Gulf and as successive diplomatic initiatives failed, fears of a worldwide terrorist onslaught against Americans and American interests in particular (as well as those of the other coalition member-states) mounted.[23] Thus, by the time the war began in January 1991, the world was primed for the possibility of retaliatory international terrorist operations which never occurred to any significant extent.

There were, admittedly, some spontaneous shows of support for Iraq by terrorists throughout the world. According to The RAND-St Andrews University Chronology of International Terrorism, for

example, 188 incidents occurred between the start of the war on 16
January 1991 and the cessation of fighting on 26 February, compared to
only 35 incidents during the same time period in 1990.[24] Only one, it
should be emphasised, targeted commercial, much less military,
aviation – passengers or otherwise.

Such attacks as did occur, were not only 'symbolic' in the sense of
terrorists attacking readily identified 'symbols' of a particular nation-
state; they were almost universally directed against 'soft' targets, not,
for example, against either airline flights or airports. Terrorists in
Ecuador, for example, stepped up their attacks on US banks and
churches there; German radicals fire-bombed a Woolworth's
department store in Bonn; guerrillas belonging to the Tupac Amaru
Revolutionary Movement in Peru attacked Kentucky Fried Chicken
outlets in that country, while terrorists in Uganda bombed an American
athletic club. The only incident that had even a passing connection to
aviation was when Islamic militants in Malaysia attempted to blow up
a downtown American Airlines ticketing office.

In summary, then, even when a massive global terrorist campaign,[25]
orchestrated by a ruthless, renegade dictator leading one of the globe's
leading 'pariah' states is mounted for stakes arguably commensurate with
the complete paralysing of worldwide aviation, commercial aircraft are
not even targeted: air cargo integrators, are not even actually threatened.
Thus, in the absence of another significant global crisis-cum-conflict,
such as the 1990-91 Gulf War, it is hard to see what motive terrorists
would have in attempting to 'paralyse' worldwide air traffic, even if this
were possible, by placing bombs in the packages transported by air cargo
integrators. In any event, where concern or suspicion might be aroused,
appropriate additional security measures can be implemented. In such
circumstances, cargo may of course be subjected to thorough inspection
and, in some instances, refused. Finally, as international air cargo
integrators in particular rely almost exclusively on their own dedicated
all-cargo aircraft, it is difficult to see how any such motive of terrorists'
to 'paralyse' international civil aviation could or even would in fact
succeed.

Conclusion

The potential threat to air cargo integrators posed by terrorists cannot be
considered high at this time. Terrorist activity against commercial

aviation in general has primarily consisted of 'symbolic' attacks against known and demonstrable 'symbols' of specific nation-states in order to call attention to political causes. Terrorists have not attacked air cargo integrators because they lack this identification or associational value, are considerably less well-known than commercial air passenger carriers and, since they do not carry passengers whose death and injury is grist for the media, do not have the same 'sensationalism' and publicity value as established passenger carriers.

Further, terrorists, because of an inherent organisational imperative, are driven towards achieving a higher margin of success in their operations than any other type of organisation or group. Simply put, if terrorists fail in an attack, they do not succeed in 'terrorising' anyone. Hence, terrorists are decidedly more imitative than they are innovative in both their tactics or targets. The fact that air cargo integrators have not previously ever been the targets of criminals (whom terrorists might aspire to imitate), or other terrorists themselves, on its own suggests that this type of potential target is at extremely low risk.

Moreover, if terrorists are obsessed with success and accordingly operationally very cautious and conservative, adhering to a narrow, but proven, tactical repertoire, they are therefore ineluctably also 'control freaks', seeking to dominate and affect all aspects of an operation in order to ensure its greatest likelihood of success. As previously recounted, the nature of the air cargo integrator, relying on speed of delivery and exploiting a variety of modes of transport whilst not adhering to a strictly scheduled time-table, obviously negates this terrorist imperative. In addition, the standardised and detailed accountability and tracking procedures of all consignments accepted by air cargo integrators acts as a further deterrent to terrorist attack given the forensic evidence and paper-trail available to law enforcement to aid its investigation of an incident. Finally, it is also worth noting that even at times of intense, extreme international tension, such as during the 1990-91 Gulf War, terrorists did not attempt to paralyse international commercial air traffic of passenger carriers, much less cargo or air cargo integrator carriers.

In conclusion, it should be emphasised that, overall, the incidence of terrorist attacks on aircraft is declining and has declined appreciably in the 1990s to the point where it accounts for 0.3 per cent of all international terrorist attacks. As I wrote in an article published in *Aviation Security*, 'Beyond a certain point, security considerations ...

can become so cumbersome as to impede the operation of the facility they are meant to protect from intrusion and interference.' This applies equally to air cargo integrators. Indeed, there is a point beyond which security measures are not only inappropriate to the level of the threat, but become so bureaucratic and illogically inconsistent, if not intellectually dishonest, that they threaten to throttle the livelihood of an entire industry with a hitherto impeccable security and safety standard. Surely, we are approaching that point with the proposed changes equating the threat to, and the attendant security measures required, regarding commercial passenger air carriers and air cargo integrators.

NOTES

1. WP/4 Report of the Task Force on Cargo Security presented to the Meeting of the Sub Group for the Study of Operational Aspects of Security Problems held at Berne contained in European Express Organisation Comments on the Report of the Task Force Submitted to the Berne Meeting (30 November to 2 December 1994).

2. For a more detailed analysis of the general threat, see Bruce Hoffman, 'Aviation Security and Terrorism', *Aviation Security International: The Journal of Airport and Airline Security*, 1/ 1 (January 1996), pp. 4-8.

3. See, for example, Brian Jenkins, *The Terrorist Threat to Commercial Aviation* (Santa Monica, CA: RAND, March 1989, P-7540); C.J. Visser (Netherlands Institute of International Relations), 'Civil Aviation and the Aircraft Bomb', Flight Safety Foundation, *Flight Safety Digest* (October 1990), pp. 1-13; 'Aviation Statistics: An Update of World-wide Airport Security System', Flight Safety Foundation, *Flight Safety Digest* (November 1989), pp. 9-12; and, E.A. 'Jerry' Jerome, 'Recent Hijackings, Bombings Accelerate Security Concerns', Flight Safety Foundation, *Flight Safety Digest* (July 1985), pp. 1-9.

4. Source: The RAND-St Andrews University Chronology of International Terrorism. The RAND-St Andrews University Chronology of International Terrorism is derived from, and is one component of, The RAND-St Andrews University Databases on Terrorism and Low-Intensity Conflict and the collection of materials on twentieth century conflict donated by Control Risks Ltd. Both of these resources consist of newspaper clippings and journal articles from more than 100 countries and in more than 5 languages. Material from The RAND-St Andrews databases is organised in nine on-line, specialised computerised 'chronologies' of terrorist incidents, where terrorist incidents and other acts of politically-motivated violence are listed in chronological format and coded for rapid data retrieval. The largest and best known of these is The RAND Chronology of International Terrorism. The Chronology contains information on international terrorist incidents since 1968 derived from the open literature (as are *all* the databases): newspapers, journals, published government reports and documents, radio broadcasts, and the foreign press. It provides a comprehensive, independent source of information with which trends in various aspects of terrorism can be analysed. It is widely acknowledged as the pre-eminent open-source (i.e., unclassified) independently maintained repository of data on terrorism worldwide.

5. 'Aviation Statistics: An Update of Worldwide Airport Security System', Flight Safety Foundation, *Flight Safety Digest* (November 1989), p. 9.

6. Statistics from the RAND-St Andrews University Chronology of International Terrorism (see note 4).

7. William Landes, 'An Economic Study of United States Aircraft Hijacking, 1966-1976', *Journal of Law and Economics*, 21 (1978), pp. 1-31.
8. Source: The RAND-St Andrews University Chronology of International Terrorism (see note 4).
9. Among the most recent incidents, for example, are: the 1985 inflight bombing of an Air India passenger jet killed all 328 persons on board; the bombing of Pan Am flight 103 in 1988 killed 278 persons; the 1989 inflight bombing of a French UTA flight killed 171; and the inflight bombing in 1989, of a Colombian Avianca aircraft on which 107 persons perished.
10. A bomb exploded in the cargo hold of an Air Lanka passenger jet whilst on the ground at Colombo Airport, Sri Lanka in 1986; Pan Am flight 103 in 1988; and a UTA passenger flight in 1989. This list refers only to bombs that were concealed in checked baggage. See *Report of the President's Commission on Aviation Security and Terrorism* (Washington, D.C., 15 May 1990, p. 166.
11. This practice has also saved airlines an estimated half a million dollars a year in compensation for lost baggage. Presentation by Rodney Wallis, former President of the International Aviation Organization, at the 'Seminar on Technology and Terrorism' held at St. Andrews University, Scotland, 24-27 August 1992.
12. A bombing in Bessarabia in 1921; a 1925 bombing of a crowded cathedral in Sofia, Bulgaria; a largely unrecorded attempt to poison imprisoned German SS concentration camp guards shortly after the Second World War; the crash of a hijacked Malaysian passenger plane in 1977; the arson attack at a Teheran movie theatre in 1979 that killed more than 400; the 1983 bombing of the US Marine barracks in Lebanon that killed 241; the aforementioned 1985 inflight bombing of an Air India passenger jet that killed all 328 persons on board; the simultaneous explosions that rocked an ammunition dump in Islamabad, Pakistan in 1988; the bombing of Pan Am flight 103 in 1988 that killed 278 persons; the 1989 inflight bombing of a French UTA flight that killed 171; the inflight bombing, as in 1989, of a Colombian Avianca aircraft on which 107 persons perished; and the 1995 bombing of the Edward P. Murrah Federal Government Office Building in Oklahoma City in which 164 persons died. As terrorism expert Brian Jenkins noted in 1985 of the list upon which the preceding is an expanded version: 'Lowering the criterion to 50 deaths produces a dozen or more additional incidents. To get even a meaningful sample, the criterion has to be lowered to 25. This in itself suggests that it is either very hard to kill large numbers of persons or very rarely tried.' Brian M. Jenkins, *The Likelihood of Nuclear Terrorism* (Santa Monica, CA: RAND, P-7119, July 1985), p. 7. This author would argue that it is the latter explanation given the terrorists' organisational imperative of success.
13. This argument is even more pertinent to air cargo integrators. See the discussion below.
14. Such as 1985 explosion at Japan's Narita Airport while baggage was being unloaded from a Canadian Pacific Airline aircraft that killed two airport workers and wounded four others
15. For example, the mixture of liquid plastic explosive concealed in a half gallon whisky jug that was triggered by a block of C-4 plastic explosive hidden in a radio that exploded in mid-air on board a Korean Airlines flight, whilst over Burma, in November 1987.
16. See Jeffrey D. Simon, *The Terrorist Trap: America's Experience with Terrorism* (Bloomington and Indianapolis: Indiana University Press, 1995), pp. 46-51.
17. According to the RAND-St Andrews University Chronology of International Terrorism, the first recorded *international terrorist* incident of inflight bombing occurred on 1 March 1969, when a bomb exploded aboard an Ethiopian Airlines Boeing 707 jet while on the ground in Frankfurt, West Germany.
18. For example, the 'trucking' of a consignment to a more geographically distant airport in order to make an earlier scheduled flight.
19. Billie H. Vincent and Robert W. Smith, 'Safeguard your cargo with new securities: enhanced technologies , such as x-rays and particle detectors, dampen illegal acts', *Air

Cargo World, 83/6 (June 1993), p. 31.
20. European Express Organisation 'Comments On the report of the Task Force Submitted to the Berne Meeting (30 November to 2 December 1994).
21. Bureau of Public Affairs, US Department of State, *Department of State Dispatch,* 5 November 1990. See also, Patrick E. Tyler and John M. Goshko, 'US Warns Iraq About Terrorism', *Washington Post*, 14 September 1990; Arthur Allen, 'Expect terror, Iraq warns', *Washington Times*, 14 September 1990; and, Marie Colvin, 'Saddam aims for supremacy in Arab world with terrorist take-over', *Sunday Times* (London), 23 September 1990. Reuters, 'Guerrilla chief orders "Hit US"', *The Guardian* (London), 16 August 1990. See also, 'Terrorist says his groups attacks if US strikes', *Washington Times,* 10 September 1990; and, Tony Horwitz, 'A Terrorist Talks About Life, Warns Of More Deaths', *Wall Street Journal*, 10 September 1990.
22. Reuters, 'Guerrilla chief orders "Hit US"' *The Guardian* (London), 16 August 1990. See also, 'Terrorist says his groups attacks if US strikes', *Washington Times,* 10 September 1990; and, Tony Horwitz, 'A Terrorist Talks About Life, Warns Of More Deaths', *Wall Street Journal*, 10 September 1990. and, Walter S. Mossberg and Gerald F. Seib, 'Before Its Invasion, Iraq Strengthened Ties To Terrorist Network', *Wall Street Journal*, 20 August 1990.
23. Peter F. Sisler, 'Terrorist threatens widening of war', *Washington Times,* 8 January 1991.
24. The US Department of State recorded 120 incidents during the war compared with 17 during the same period of time in 1990. In any event, so huge an increase is extremely uncommon.
25. Ibid.; Michael Wines, 'International Teamwork May Have Foiled Terror', *New York Times*, 4 March 1991; Harvey Elliot, 'Security agencies link up to tackle international threat', *The Times* (London), 30 January 1991; and, Peter Grier, 'Terrorist Impact In US Still Small', *Christian Science Monitor* (Boston), 8 August 1991. See also the testimony of Mr. Ken Bergquist, Associate Director of the US State Department's Office of Counter-Terrorism before the US Senate Committee on Governmental Affairs, 16 July 1991; and, Ambassador L. Paul Bremmer's speech to the Institute for East-West Security Studies on 11 April 1991 as reported in the Institute's newsletter.

6

The Missile Threat to Civil Aviation

MARVIN B. SCHAFFER

The historical record since the invention and fielding of heat-seeking missiles in the late 1960s supports the assertion that they can knock large passenger aircraft out of the sky. Early designs were marginal in their target discrimination, range, altitude and maneuverability capabilities, but they have been steadily improved. Recent systems have the ability to engage targets up to altitudes of more than 20,000 feet and can attack from any direction. Specifically, they do not have to see hot engines or their exhaust, but can engage disparate areas on the aircraft fuselage or wings. We will trace the evolution of man-portable missiles including their successful use by terrorist groups against civilian aircraft to support our belief that they are a threat both now and in the future. Finally, we will outline some measures that could and should be taken to alleviate that threat.

On the tenth anniversary of the Pan Am 103 crash over Lockerbie, Scotland, it is certainly appropriate to reassess the terrorist threat to civilian aviation. The record indicates that although missile shootdowns are less likely then airport bombings, hi-jacking, or attacks on aircraft with explosive booby-traps, they nevertheless have been occurring at rates of up to once or twice a year for more than twenty years and cannot be ignored.

The Man-Portable Missile Threat

The first thing to know about man-portable missiles is that there are hundreds of thousands of them in many arsenals throughout the world, and thousands are believed to be in the hands of terrorist groups. There are two basic varieties: infrared-seeking and beam riders. They have been fielded in *nineteen* different configurations beginning in 1967 – twelve of the infrared and seven of the beam rider variety. Tables 1 and 2 identify these missiles along with their countries of origin, range and altitude. The principal developers and exporters of infrared missiles are the CIS (Russia), the USA, and France. The UK and Sweden have produced beam riders.

Note that the two lists are by no means exhaustive. At least four other countries – China, North Korea, Egypt and Pakistan – produce domestic infrared missiles for their inventories that appear to be copies of Russian, French or US missiles. Other countries have imported missiles, and then proceeded to export them. As we elaborate on below, man-portable anti-aircraft missiles currently can be purchased in any of several dozen countries.

TABLE 1
INFRARED-SEEKING MISSILES

System	Country	Range (Ft)	Altitude (Ft)	Year
Redeye	US	13,800	8,900	1967
SA-7a	USSR	14,100	9,900	1968
SA-7b	USSR	16,400	14,800	1972
SA-14	USSR	18,000	15,400	1978
Stinger	US	18,000	15,400	1981
SA-16	USSR	22,600	22,600	1981
SA-18	USSR	22,600	22,600	1984
Stinger POST	US	20,700	15,400	1986
Mistral	France	22,300	21,300	1989
Stinger RMP	US	20,700	15,400	1990
SA-18 (IGLA D)	Russia	22,600	22,600	1994
Keiko II	Japan	19,700	13,100	1995

TABLE 2
BEAM-RIDER MISSILES

System	Country	Range (Ft)	Altitude (Ft)	Year
Blowpipe	UK	12,100	8,200	1975
RBS-70, Mk I	Sweden	16,400	9,800	1977
Javelin	UK	18,000	9,800	1984
RBS-70, Mk II	Sweden	23,000	23,000	1988
Starburst	UK	18,000	9,800	1990
RBS-90	Sweden	23,000	16,400	1991
Starstreak	UK	16,400	16,400	1993

The original systems, and those best known to observers of the Vietnam War era, were the US Redeye and the Russian SA-7, the latter fielded in several variations. Improvements in the form of three versions of the US Stinger, and three Russian missiles, the SA-14, SA-16, SA-18 followed. They were subsequently joined by the French Mistral and the Japanese Keiko II. These eight designs are now the dominant infrared missile systems in the sense that they are highly capable and widely available in good condition. Capable beam-rider missile systems also exist: namely RBS-70 Mk II, RBS-90, and Starstreak.

Man-portable missiles have proliferated worldwide as a result of sales, grants and licenses from government or private entities in the nine principal manufacturing countries. Some 56 countries are known to be in possession of the SA-7 missile alone, and dozens more own stockpiles of one or more of the others. Stinger variations are owned by 20 countries other than the US. The SA-14 has been exported to 32 countries, the SA-16 to 41 countries, and the SA-18 is owned by Bosnia, Brazil and India in addition to Russia. More than 100,000 SA-7/14 missiles were exported by Russia, and some 9,000 Stinger variations by the USA. The Afghan guerrillas were given about 750 Stingers by the USA, and used them to shoot down more than 100 Soviet aircraft. In 1993, the mojahedin still possessed several hundred Stingers.

It is not surprising that man-portable missiles have found their way into the hands of the world's terrorist groups. When regional wars or wars of liberation end or lapse, governments and other groups sorely in need of hard currency tend to sell their unused weapon stockpiles on the open market. With that process ongoing since the 1980s, at least 17 terrorist or insurgent groups have acquired man-portable missiles; they are listed in Table 3. Some of these groups are well-financed, implying they would not hesitate to pay handsomely for the highest technology available. Others would probably opt for the cheapest weapons offered.

To put the missile threat in the right context without overstating the case, we will briefly review the record on terrorist acts in general. In 1993, RAND estimated that more than 8,000 terrorist incidents had been perpetrated worldwide since 1968, 40 per cent more in the 1980s than the 1970s. Only a fraction were directed against the world's airlines: 12 per cent in the 1980s, and 21 per cent in the 1970s. According to the RAND-St. Andrews Chronology, there were 484

TABLE 3
TERRORIST OR INSURGENT GROUPS WITH MAN-PORTABLE MISSILES

Terrorist or Insurgent Group	Country
Irish Republican Army (Ira)	No. Ireland
Kurdistan Workers' Party (Pkk)	Turkey
Nat. Union For Total Lib. Of Angola (UNITA)	Angola
Afghan Mojahedin	Afghanistan
Contras, Sandinistas	Nicaragua
Warring Factions	Bosnia-Herzegovina
Farabundo Marti National Lib. Front (Fmln)	El Salvador
Chechen Rebels	Chechnia
Tamil Tigers	Sri Lanka
Warring Factions	Somalia
GIA	Algeria
AMAL, Hezbollah, And PLO	Lebenon
Rwandan Patriotic Front	Rwanda
Sudanese People's Liberation Army (SPLA)	Sudan
Iranian Revolutionary Guards	Iran
South West African People's Organization	Namibia
Kmer Rouge	Cambodia

terrorist incidents in 1991, 343 in 1992, 360 in 1993, and 350 in 1994. Although these were below the levels of the 1980s, the lethal toll was higher. In 1994, the lethal toll was 423 civilian deaths, the fifth highest since 1968. The 1994 record included 22 attacks on the airline industry (6.3 per cent of the total), including two terrorist missile attacks, one successful and one unsuccessful.

The incidence rate of one or two man-portable missile attacks per year has been occurring more or less continuously since 1985, and sporadically for the decade preceding that. The rate of these attacks, compiled from media accounts, is summarized in Figure 1. Included are confirmed attacks where the aircraft was downed and/or casualties resulted, unsuccessful attacks which were either thwarted beforehand or missed, and suspected but unconfirmed attacks. Most of these events occurred in environments where active fighting was underway. Typically, a successful attack kills about 19 civilians. Thus, while missile-related terrorist incidents are only a small fraction of the total, they can result in great loss of life.

Technological Evolvement

A short review of man-portable missile technology is appropriate since recent designs are not very familiar to the general public. Man-portable

FIGURE 1
MAN-PORTABLE MISSILE ATTACKS ON CIVILIAN AIRCRAFT

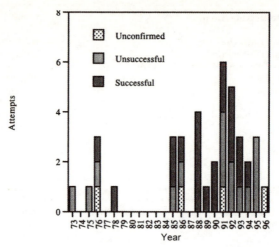

missiles have progressed through three design generations, and a fourth is on the drawing boards. Recent designs are much more capable than the original versions. Improvements in range and altitude, as shown in Tables 1 and 2, were matched by increases in missile speed (from 1900 f/s in 1967 to 2800 f/s in 1996), and maneuverability (from 13 gs to 32 gs). Most importantly, seeker and tracking technologies now permit the exploitation of more useful portions of the electromagnetic spectrum, and use more reliable signal processing techniques. The evolution of these characteristics is displayed in Figure 2. Early systems, such as Redeye and the SA-7, detected solar reflections and hot metal using uncooled lead sulfide elements and AM tracking logic. The next generation (Stinger and SA-14/16) used cooled indium/antimony elements to detect hot metal and engine plume exhaust while tracking with FM logic. A third generation typified by Stinger POST/RMP and the SA-18 employs dual-band seeker elements, while the Keiko II seeker employs a focal-plane-array, full imaging configuration.

The net result of the technology improvements is that newer generations of manportable missiles have the ability to engage targets at altitudes up to 20,000 feet within a substantially wider envelope of speeds and directional approaches. Specifically, they can engage targets frontally or from the side or rear. Moreover, they are relatively insensitive to flare countermeasures. Focal-plane-array seekers also have the potential for resistance to laser countermeasures (although the

FIGURE 2
IR GUIDANCE AND TRACKING CHARACTERISTICS

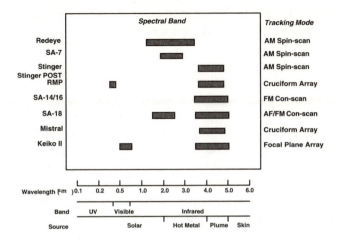

Keiko II apparently has not fully exploited that feature) and the ability to select impact points anywhere on the aircraft. Additionally, current research is focusing on seeker wavelengths above 5 microns, which will enable tracking aerodynamically heated aircraft skin, further enhancing the all-aspect engagement capability.

Are Large, Multi-Engined Aircraft Vulnerable to IR Missiles?

The short answer is yes. However, the reliability of early missile generations was probably of the order of only 15–20 per cent, indicating that simultaneous attacks with as many as three or four missiles were warranted for efficient operation. SA-7 missiles, which have proliferated most on a worldwide basis, suffer from unreliable fuzing, susceptibility to being confused by sun glare, relatively short range, low altitude engagement capabilities, limited target speeds, and constrained seeker sensitivity. Moreover, they are limited to only tail chases. Although definitive data are not in the public domain, more recent missile generations have been improved across the board and are expected to be much more reliable.

Questions have also been raised about whether it is even possible for a missile warhead with a 4–5 lb warhead containing only 1–2 lbs of explosive to shoot down or seriously disrupt a large transport aircraft. Although the historical record largely speaks for itself in the affirmative, we would emphasize that the crucial determining factor is where on the aircraft the missile or its explosive debris hits. Specifically:

- Aircraft have many points of vulnerability to explosive trauma. A 1lb explosive detonation in or near a fuel tank, for example, would most likely cause a massive explosion, depending on the fuel-oxygen mixture, and if not an explosion, a fire. A detonation which severs critical non-redundant cables can cause the pilot to lose control of the aircraft. Damage to critical control surfaces can have a similar effect. A detonation which causes explosive loss of an engine or which tears a substantial gap in a wing or fuselage could cause large asymmetric yaw or pitch moments which might also result in loss of control.
- Engagement speeds of man-portable missiles are typically Mach 1.5 to 2. Depending on whether the engagement is a head-on or tail chase, the net impact speed would be in the Mach 1 to 2.5 bracket (as high as 3000 f/s). The kinetic energy of impact of a 20lb, frangible bullet at those speeds might be sufficient in and of itself to cause an explosion or to tear large holes in the aircraft structure; it is roughly the effective equivalent of a 90mm anti-tank projectile.
- Even if the aircraft is hit and not downed, the jolt, turbulence and/or loss of cabin pressure might be sufficient to kill or injure crew or passengers.
- The unfortunate fact is that systematic work to develop frequency of impact maps for man-portable missiles against the world's commercial aircraft has not been done and reliable data do not exist. It is not a trivial task to infer where the impact will be for a specific geometric engagement. A widely held belief is that the missiles always hit hot engines, but that is not necessarily the case.
- When a missile engages in a tail chase, as the Redeyeor SA-7 do and other missiles can do, its seeker sees several hot spots from the engines and plumes. As it closes on the target, the field of view shrinks and the number of hot spots in view shrink. Eventually, it gets to a point where only one or two hot spots show, and the missile seeker ultimately focuses in that area. Will there be enough time to hit the selected area or will the missile impact between or near the

hot spots? It depends on the dynamics and maneuverability of the missile; the answer is not obvious and requires testing for resolution.

- When a missile engages head-on, as more recent missiles can do, the infrared scene is entirely different. The engines may or may not be visible. The leading edge of the wings and/or fuselage will probably dominate the picture. Where will a missile impact? It will select the area where the average infrared return is strongest, and try to focus on that spot as it gets closer. Again, the impact point will depend on the dynamics and maneuverability of the missile.
- When a missile engages from the side, the image characteristics will be a mixture of the above. The expected impact point again requires testing for resolution.
- If countermeasures such as flares or offset 'hotspot' decoys are involved, the picture is further complicated.

The dynamics of a tail chase are as follows. Four engines/plumes are initially in view. As the missile gets closer, two engines are lost from view and the missile seeker turns so that the remaining hot spots are centered. However, the missile cannot complete its turn, and impacts alongside one inboard engine. This, of course, is not necessarily what happens. The missile may hit one of the engines, or it may impact between the two engines.

The 'tests' referred to involve hardware-in-the-loop simulations where actual missile seekers are exposed to replications of the aircraft infrared image. The seeker is mounted on gimbals and constrained in pitch and yaw duplicating the engagement dynamics; that is, it is given overturning moments from simulated control surfaces. Such simulations are a well-developed concept, and have been used for years by the US Navy to develop expected impact maps against military aircraft. Extension to commercial aircraft maps is straightforward but, to the knowledge of the author, has not been done.

What Can Be Done?

There are a number of countermeasures that can be applied to man-portable missiles which would reduce the risk to commercial aviation if adopted. They can be classified into passive and active categories. Some are relatively inexpensive but only partially effective. The most effective active countermeasure, a missile warning system (MWS) plus a laser jammer, would cost about 2 billion dollars if installed on the entire US widebody fleet; the least effective passive countermeasure systems might cost 100 times less than that, or about 20 million dollars. The wide disparity in cost-effectiveness between the options is the reason we need to develop impact maps as a matter of priority. If systematic mapping is done, it may be possible to install a much less costly mixture of passive and active countermeasures with a substantial reduction in susceptibility and vulnerability to missile attack.

Passive Countermeasures

- Infrared Signature Reduction. Once an understanding is gained of where impacts are expected, one can consider a systematic reduction or alteration of an aircraft's infrared image. Such efforts might amount to shielding, special paints, and/or a mixture of cold airstream with hot plume gases. Infrared signature reduction or alteration techniques are among the least expensive countermeasures, and are employed routinely on military aircraft. They should prove effective against early-generation man-portable missile designs but possibly not against the later generations
- Offset decoys. Use of offset infrared decoys is a special case of signature alteration. It is conceivable that offset sources could cause attacking missiles to miss entirely or to result in greatly reduced damage. We envisage attaching emitting devices separated from the aircraft structure by only a few feet so as to minimize the alteration of the drag field. The Israeli Air Force implemented a representative modification kit on A-4 aircraft in the early 1970s known as 'stovepipe' which worked quite well against the threats of the time. Recoverable, offset decoys ought to be less expensive than flares, and less objectionable, since nothing is ejected from the aircraft.
- Fuel Tank Inerting. A number of schemes have been considered to reduce the potential for explosion and fire in fuel tanks, including reticulated foam and self-sealing bladders. The most promising and one that is receiving current study is inerting the tank with a nitrogen atmosphere. Nitrogen inerting is used in Apache helicopters, and will also be used in Comanche. Fuel tank inerting has a utility well beyond missile countermeasures; it could produce a significant reduction in the incidence of fuel fire from accidental ignition sources.
- Redundant controls. A well-established principle for minimizing the effects of missile attack and explosions in general is to utilize

redundant controls with separation. It is a principle that has not been routinely adhered to. For example, most commercial and military aircraft depend on common data bus wiring. A critically located explosion could therefore take out virtually all the avionics; this may be what happened to TWA 800. Newer aircraft, currently being designed, use digital avionics and have an opportunity for effective redundancy. The Boeing 777, Airbus 340, F-22, and JSF aircraft all fall into this category

Active Countermeasures

- ATIRCMS. The Advanced Threat Infrared Countermeasures System is a multi-service program to provide man-portable missile protection to the US Army's fleet of helicopters, the US Air Force/Navy/Marine fleets of fighters, and potentially to US military transport aircraft. ATIRCMS has four major subsystems: a missile warning system (MWS) using both the UV portion of the spectrum to detect ground launches and the mid-IR portion to track the missile after burnout, a xenon lamp to jam high-frequency/low wavelength threats, and a solid-state laser to jam 3-5 micronmid-wavelength infrared threats. ATIRCMS, as presently envisioned, weighs about 125lbs, and is due to be fielded in the year 2000. Commercial aviation observers are skeptical about ATIRCMS' utility for civilian transports because of the cost (presently estimated at $1 million), the weight penalty, and the fact that it uses a laser (albeit low power) which could cause blinding injuries. However, development tests indicate that ATIRCMS is thus far the most effective countermeasure against the man-portable missile threat including the more recent design generations.
- DIRCM. The Directed Infrared Countermeasure system is a less effective system but is currently in production, several years before ATIRCMS. Instead of a laser, it employs an upgraded xenon lamp to jam oncoming missile seekers. DIRCM also uses a UV/IR MWS to acquire and track target missiles. It is slated to be fielded on USAFSOC C-130 aircraft initially, and is also being considered by the British Ministry of Defense for fighter aircraft. The weight is about 195lbs, but the cost is considerably less than that of ATIRCMS. If a near-term requirement arose for commercial transports, DIRCM might well be the system of choice because it is off-the-shelf and relatively affordable. However, although it

performs well against early-generation infrared missiles, it is ineffective against late-generation systems.

- Flares. The use of chemical flares is a well-established countermeasure against heat-seeking missiles. Flares have been used extensively in military aircraft, and in fact work reasonably well against early-generation missiles. However, later-generation missiles (Stinger POST/RMP, SA-18) incorporate logic that recognizes and distinguishes flare trajectories, and filters out their images. Flares have also occasionally been used by Israeli commercial aircraft during landings and takeoffs in dangerous environments. Their use, however, is not considered an acceptable practice to most of the international aviation community because of their high visibility and the fact that they call attention to the missile threat.

Long-Term Measures

Another approach for reducing the man-portable missile threat is to devise and implement a system of international controls. These could take the form of diplomatic actions and/or new innovative hardware and software. For example:

- An agreement to establish international controls against man-portable SAM proliferation. Enforcement protocols might include establishment and recording of inventories and sales of shoulder-fired missiles at a neutral registry. Enhancements could include appropriate security for existing stocks, and notification to oversight groups of any thefts.
- Buy up the world supply of man-portable missiles at market prices. Unfortunately, previous attempts to buy excess Stingers from Afghan guerrillas in the early 1990s were only marginally successful.
- Develop enabling and disabling locks for future missiles. These techniques have been used successfully for nuclear weapons, and the same technologies could be applied without large penalizing weight increases.
- An agreement that prevents the blatant use of civilian aircraft to ferry troops or material into theaters of conflict. If it is required that such aircraft be recommissioned and repainted as military aircraft, it is less likely that commercial aircraft in the vicinity would be attacked.

The Future

Effective solutions to the man-portable missile problem, although expensive, are clearly in the public interest. Unfortunately, if history is the judge, nothing significant will be done unless and until there is an unambiguous, catastrophic shootdown either in the USA or in Europe. If that occurs (and it is most probable if not inevitable), we predict a series of expedient 'fixes' to be undertaken, along with much more intensive study of the problem. Among the expected expedient countermeasures are:

- Strengthened security in the vicinity of airfields. Since the areas involved are hundreds of square miles at each site, and the number of airfields number in the tens of thousands, this will be a token effort probably at a few international airports.
- Reduced take-off and landing pattern areas. During the Vietnam conflict, for example, Pan Am flights into Ton Sonhut Airport in Saigon used steep spiral descents greatly decreasing the 50-mile exposure during normal approach. Takeoff exposures could also be shortened, although to a lesser extent. This type of measure significantly decreases the magnitude of the threat, but is disruptive to efficient patterns of commercial traffic and would probably be used only sparingly.
- Increased night flying with shielded lights. A man-portable missile shooter must first see the target as a prerequisite to getting an infrared lock-on. Aircraft lights normally make this much easier for the unaided eye. It is conceivable that a terrorist team could be equipped with night vision optics, but the effective viewing ranges are short, typically a few thousand feet.

Sooner or later, the world's commercial aviation fleets will incorporate equipment in some form to negate the threat of man-portable missiles. As we have suggested, technology for accomplishing this is fairly advanced in a military context, and much of that technology is applicable to the civilian fleet. We believe it is now in the public interest to undertake a definitive program of action to develop and stockpile such equipment without waiting for a new, catastrophic event to occur. In addition, there are substantial issues of a policy nature that need to be treated, and resolution of those issues should be in the vanguard of an improvement program. Specifically:

- The man-portable missile threat to commercial aviation is an international problem. What is the appropriate international forum? If the United Nations is the agency, the US delegation could and should take the lead in introducing an action resolution.
- As the world's leading operator and producer of commercial aircraft, what role should US industry play in creating new policy? Their participation is essential because eventually they will be called upon to retrofit their existing fleet and to provide equipment for new aircraft.
- Who will pay for countermeasures to the man-portable missile terrorist threat? If it is clear to the aviation industry worldwide that it is an international effort and that they will not have to bear the brunt of the cost, their support would be enhanced if not assured.

The persistent theme and recommendation of this paper is that future studies and expedient actions would be 'jump-started' if reliable data existed describing expected impact points for man-portable missiles against commercial multi-engined aircraft, both narrow body and wide body. A systematic program of mapping could be completed for a fraction of the cost of protective hardware. The threat record supports that undertaking on an international basis.

7

The Role of the International Aviation Organisations in Enhancing Security

RODNEY WALLIS

From the time of their joint conception in 1946, two aviation bodies have dominated international civil aviation. They are the International Civil Aviation Organization (ICAO – the aviation wing of the United Nations) and the International Air Transport Association (IATA), the trade association of the world's scheduled airlines. Both have their headquarters in Montreal, Canada.

When airborne terrorism first threatened commercial air services, both organisations rose to the challenge and today's international standards and recommended practises published in ICAO's Annex 17 (Security) to the Chicago Convention on International Civil Air Transport, and IATA's own resolutions contained in their Passenger Conference and Security Manuals, owe their origins to this early reaction.

ICAO and IATA remain at the forefront of international aviation rule-making but in the current decade, as IATA's public voice on security matters has become muted, more has been heard of a third body with the potential to influence the air transport industry's response to airborne terrorism. This is the Geneva-based Airports Council International (ACI), formed by the merger in 1991 of the Airport Operators Council International (a US-dominated airport group) and the International Civil Airports Association (principally a European organization). Under an earlier umbrella heading of the Airports Association Co-ordinating Council, these two groups provided important input to the decision making processes at the UN agency. However, for the most part, their early efforts were limited to the activities of a committed minority of specialist volunteers drawn from members of the two constituent associations.

One other international organisation exists which has the ability to enhance aviation security. The European Civil Aviation Conference (ECAC) is a subordinate body to ICAO and regional in its responsibility; however, four of its member states, UK, France, Germany and Italy, are G7 powers and permanent members of the ICAO Council. The USA and Canada, both members of the G7, have permanent observer status at ECAC meetings while the balance of states making up the regional body's membership are mainly industrial powers with a level of affluence superior to that achieved by the average ICAO Contracting State. This has meant that in security terms, the level at which security standards can be set – the common denominator – is considerably higher within ECAC than that which can be achieved by ICAO. The latter has to allow for the economic and management weaknesses so often indigenous to the civil aviation authorities of the developing world. Even so, ECAC shares a common weakness with the UN body – neither is able to enforce its rules on its members. Indeed in the area of security implementation, the four organisations have this feature in common. They are associations of sovereign entities and have no powers of compliance over their members.

Given the foregoing what, in practise, is the role of the international aviation organisations in enhancing civil aviation security?

ICAO

The International Civil Aviation Organization comprises 185 contracting (member) states (June, 1997). It derives its mandate from the 1944 Conference on International Civil Aviation as does IATA, although the airline body was officially brought into being by an act of the Canadian Parliament. ICAO was formally born when the appropriate number of states ratified the treaty developed in Chicago. Through a tiered committee structure, ICAO develops and publishes International Standards (mandatory rules) and Recommended Practises, which its member states are urged to implement.

At the conceptual level within ICAO, the Aviation Security Panel, a specialist body drawing its membership from a number of states and international organizations, creates the required mandatory rules and guidelines. The group was inaugurated in 1985 following the bombing of an Air India Boeing 747 over the Atlantic when more than 300 persons died. At that time, the Panel was specifically charged with reviewing international security standards and re-writing Annex 17 to the Chicago Convention. Annex 17 is the rule book of aviation security. The resulting work achieved by the Panel remains the basis of today's international security regulations.

Annex 17 spells out, in the form of standards and recommended practices (SARPS), the rules needed to effect a valid security programme. It is a small, singularly simple publication but one born out of much debate. It is a compromise document designed to balance the needs of civil aviation seen through the eyes of security specialists (the Panel) with political and economic considerations demanded by the wide-ranging membership of ICAO.

ICAO's use of the term 'mandatory' in relation to 'standard' requires explanation. The Organisation has no enforcement powers over its members thus, whilst ICAO Annexes are 'binding' on governments, provision is made for contracting states to opt out of regulations which, for one reason or another, they find unacceptable.

All governments are able to participate in the ICAO debates which lead to international rule-making, or to comment upon the published proposals resulting from such debates before they become effective, but many fail to do so. Representatives may attend sessions where rules are developed, and even vote for their adoption, but delegates at international meetings may vote with the mood of meeting only to have second thoughts on their return home. ICAO debates are conducted in one of five languages with instantaneous translation into the other four. The five are English, French, Spanish, Russian and Arabic. Many delegates have a first language other than one of these and thus are forced into debating terms which may be unfamiliar to them. Reflection and an opportunity for discussion in home surroundings can bring a change of position. It can also be that the representative may not have the authority or influence on his return to implement a decision taken collectively at ICAO. It may also be that the state disagreed all along but chose not to express its opinion in open forum.

Despite the foregoing, ICAO's provision of debating chambers (the Panel, the intermediary Committee on Unlawful Interference and the governing Council) in which security matters can be discussed by its Contracting States is vital to the enhancement of aviation security standards. There are signs that the Organization is attempting to strengthen its role. In May, 1997, Dr Assad Kotaite, the ICAO

President, introduced the Organisation's first ever strategic action plan which, reflecting a weakness of the Organization, had taken 'several years' to develop! The action plan covers all aspects of ICAO's work but cites in particular 'unlawful interference'. ICAO wants to be empowered to audit member states routinely for compliance with international security regulations and to 'become the recognized worldwide auditor for security standards for international civil aviation'. This would allow ICAO to assume a role IATA had fulfilled throughout the previous two decades. It meets the intentions of the civil aviation ministers who attended an extraordinary meeting of the ICAO Council eight years earlier following the Lockerbie tragedy.[1]

An enhancement of international aviation security rules and procedures can normally be linked to a major disaster which cynics may consider a case of 'shutting the stable door after the horse has bolted'. The immediate reaction of ICAO to the Air India tragedy in 1985 is one example. Activity subsequent to the loss of Pan Am's *Maid of the Seas* over Lockerbie in December 1988, is another. Following the latter, the specially convened meeting of ICAO's governing Council already mentioned provided an opportunity for behind-the-scenes negotiations among the major powers with an interest in civil aviation security. This culminated in a resolution which led to help from the wealthier countries in strengthening the structure of ICAO. The latter received support in terms of cash and manpower enabling them to introduce field operations which the Organisation determined should take the form of reviewing security standards in place at the less fiscally sound states. ICAO converted the intelligence they gathered into a training programme which is now available to its contracting states. In November 1997, ICAO took a further step forward, inaugurating a dedicated aviation security institute in Brussels thus increasing the potential for the Organisation to obtain better compliance with its security recommendations.

Part of the activity proposed by the ICAO president involves the development of a new legal instrument on air carrier liability. It will modernize the current liability regime which is based on the Warsaw Convention of 1929. This Convention limits passenger compensation following aircraft accidents, including those resulting from acts of unlawful interference, to £75,000 unless, as in the case of Pan Am, the air carrier is found guilty of wilful misconduct in respect of the incident. In such instances, the Warsaw limits of liability are waived. Individual settlements following Lockerbie rose as high as $19 million. The judge hearing the families' charges against Pan Am ruled that wilful misconduct was:

> The intentional performance of an act with knowledge that performance of that act will probably result in injury or damage, or it may be the intentional performance of an act in such a manner as to imply disregard of the probable consequences of the performance of the act
>
> Likewise, the intentional omission of some act with knowledge that such omission will probably result in damages or injury, or the intentional omission of some act in a manner from which could be implied reckless disregard of the probable consequences of the omission, would also be wilful misconduct.

The new ICAO instrument was scheduled to be studied by the Organisation's Legal Committee in the early summer of 1997 and presented to a diplomatic conference for formal adoption 'as soon as possible' after the former group had completed its work. Revision of the Warsaw provisions should help overcome the difficulties experienced by those seeking compensation in the event of an accident or death following an act of unlawful interference. However, any effect of the ICAO initiatives is unlikely to be noticed until the new millennium. It will, of course, remain the prerogative of Contracting States to accept of refuse any of the new conditions.

As this text was being developed, ICAO's role in enhancing civil aviation security had necessarily concentrated on the development of standard rules and guidelines. If implemented, these would provide a consistent and appropriate level of security worldwide. A combination of three ICAO products – Annex 17; a Security Manual containing operating guidelines; and Training Programmes – should enable any state to develop its own efficient response to terrorism aimed against civil aviation. Three other ICAO products, the Tokyo, Hague and Montreal Conventions, provide the basis for international law in respect of acts of unlawful interference.

Unhappily, despite ICAO's efforts, *effective* security exists in only a minority of countries around the world. It is frequently missing even from those states which comprise ICAO's governing council. ICAO's strategic action plan has the potential to overcome this shortcoming, but to do so it will have to effectively promote its products around the world. Practise has shown that it will require hard work to persuade many states to enhance their individual security effort.

IATA

The International Air Transport Association (IATA) membership comprises more than 200 airlines worldwide. They range from the biggest carriers to small inter-island airlines; from one end of the alphabet to the other, Aeroflot to Zambia Airways.

IATA was first established in 1919 as the International Air Traffic Association. It was reborn during the 1944 Chicago Conference on International Air Transport. In 1945 the Canadian Parliament, acting on behalf of the world's governments, gave the Association its current charter. Among the principal goals included in its Articles of Association was the requirement to:

> To promote *safe, regular and economical* air transport for the benefit of the peoples of the world, to foster air commerce and to study the problems connected therewith.

Another mandate was:

> To co-operate with the International Civil Aviation Organization and other international organizations.

With the upsurge of terrorism in the 1960s, the IATA Director General, a Swedish diplomat, Knut Hammarskjold, established a Security Advisory Committee (SAC) within the Association. For twenty years, the SAC developed collective airline policies for combating aviation terrorism. Under Hammarskjold's leadership, IATA adopted a resolution which required that :

> During and/or after actual incidents of air piracy,... (IATA)...through the Director General intervene, as necessary, with individual states when such states fail to apply the conditions of the Conventions and where IATA involvement may result in a faster resolution of the situation.

This direction separates the role of IATA from ICAO and indeed from ECAC. IATA has a mandate to intervene during on-going acts of unlawful interference and in post-incident investigations. It provided a basis for the author of this paper (then IATA's Director, Facilitation and

Security), encouraged by the Director General, to promote the use of teams of specialists to investigate incidents on-site following acts of unlawful interference. The intent of the investigations was two-fold; firstly to identify where and how the security breach had occurred, and secondly to see what lessons could be learned and applied in the future, not just at the location where the incident occurred but elsewhere on the commercial airlines' network.

By its physical involvement, IATA created an opportunity to become directly engaged in enhancing security operations around the world. The Association established a series of minimum criteria for securing airports against acts of terrorism and inaugurated a complimentary programme of surveys to test an airport's defence against acts of unlawful interference. These surveys proved to be an exceptionally well received part of IATA's work throughout the 1980s. They are still being conducted but changes in IATA policy during the past few years has led to a diminution in the frequency of visits.

Airports selected for review under the IATA programme range from heavily utilised but primarily holiday destinations to major business locations. The same criteria are used in the assessment of all the airports, but local conditions, political environments and fiscal possibilities all help to shape the recommendations which result from the surveys. Survey teams work within the IATA framework of securing *safe, regular and economical* air transport.

Locations surveyed by IATA are generally nominated by airlines operating to the location because of their concern at what they perceive to be poor standards. On occasions, an airport authority will approach IATA asking for a review. In either event, the study is always undertaken with the full agreement of the authority concerned (sometimes requiring heavy pressure being placed on the targeted authority) and at no cost to that body. This is not an altruistic action on the part of IATA or its members. It is simply a cost-effective way of ensuring that airlines serving a particular airport are afforded the maximum protection against terrorist attacks.

Teams participating in the IATA survey programme are international in their construction and, depending upon the size of the airport under examination, comprise three to four experts drawn from the airlines serving the airport or who have an interest in the region. They are normally co-ordinated and led by a member of the IATA security secretariat. This configuration has a number of advantages, not least the avoidance of national bias in the study. In effect, the teams conduct a vulnerability assessment, identifying areas of weakness and proposing changes to enhance the overall security of the air transport operation at the location being studied.

The IATA survey programme may have been the most influential activity in enhancing security operations around the world and, in part, may be responsible for the reduction in international acts of unlawful interference. Certainly the programme was endorsed by the Council of Europe who referred to it as the *'only objective survey programme available to the industry and to governments'*. The 1989, the special meeting of the ICAO Council, attended by a myriad of air transport ministers from the major Contracting States, also subscribed to the IATA programme by urging ICAO to adopt a similar approach. ICAO's new initiatives outlined their strategic action plan may well follow the pattern of the IATA activity.

IATA has introduced a number of initiatives seeking to enhance civil aviation security. They have included the development of the sterile lounge concept which now operates at the majority of the world's major airports. This concept requires passengers and their hand baggage to be screened prior to entering a sterile area and all other persons and items entering the area to be authorised and subjected to security control.

The central screening/sterile lounge concept places a distance barrier between the potential discovery of a would-be hijacker and his ultimate target, the aircraft. It allows time for police or other forces to respond to an incident before the criminal has an opportunity of reaching his goal. If screening takes place at the departure gate, it becomes a much more simple matter for the terrorist to achieve his objective. At the gate, if the terrorist believes there is a danger of his weapons being identified, he uses them at that point and in a matter of steps, reach the aircraft. 'One gate, one flight security' simplifies the terrorists task of striking his target.

Effective passenger and hand baggage screening (the most visible security procedure at an airport) requires teams of personnel (ICAO's early recommendation was for a minimum of five persons for each such operation) to be present for each aircraft departure. An airport with 20 outbound aircraft movements in an hour would need 100 persons to be on duty during the lead up period to the departure, assuming each control point was manned to the ICAO specification. In practise, during the early stages of the departure process, passengers arrive in small numbers with sizeable time gaps between them thus under-utilizing the staff. Nearer to the aircraft leaving, the numbers increase which causes queuing, often leading to a delay in the departure. With a central screening system linked to the sterile lounge concept, the same 20 departures can be handled with four check points, supplemented as and when demand warrants. This allows a manageable flow of passengers and provides major savings in personnel. It has to be remembered that unless a government authority is picking up the cost of security thus placing the burden on taxpayers, the airline passenger will eventually pay for any waste of personnel and equipment through the price of the airline ticket. The sterile lounge concept minimizes the potential for passengers to become enmeshed in security checks at a time aircraft are boarding. It also provides greater freedom of movement to passengers once they have passed security control points.

Airports quickly warmed to the policy because it enabled them to expand the provision of duty free shopping outlets. The shopping mall appearance of so many of today's major airports owe their existence to the sterile lounge concept. These facilities are popular with passengers and provide a vital source of income for the airports. Once again the IATA mandate to promote *safe, regular and economical* can be seen to be working. This commercial activity does not present opportunities for terrorists to exploit, providing the responsible authorities adopt the security control methods which were developed alongside the sterile lounge philosophy. Such operations are tested during the currency of IATA surveys.

The sterile lounge concept is an example of 'facilitation' (trying to make things simple and better for both the airline customer and the operator) and 'security' working together for the enhancement of security standards and for the physical and fiscal benefit of the air traveller. With so much of IATA's effort to raise security standards necessarily being covert, the sterile lounge concept, with its overt passenger and hand baggage screening check points, is probably the most visible of IATA's endeavours to enhance aviation security.

From the commencement of terrorist activity aimed against civil aviation operations, IATA's secretariat adopted the role of initiating new thinking to counter airborne terrorism. In 1984, long before ICAO began work on its training guidelines, IATA established residential security training sessions. It was part of the Association's attempt to support the development of air transport in developing nations that had neither the resources nor the capability of effecting valid security training programmes on their own.

The residential security training courses were supported by training officers and lecturers drawn from the IATA Secretariat and from among the security experts within the major airlines. These were supplemented by government tutors with specialisation in such subjects as explosives identification and threat assessment. Although originally intended as a service to the airlines of the developing world, several of the larger international carriers and certain civil aviation authorities quickly recognized the benefits of using the courses to train their newly appointed security executives. The programme has continued into the 1990s with area programmes serving the Asia/Pacific, Central/South American and European regions.

In 1988, IATA again broke new ground. Still pursuing its role as the initiator of new security policy thinking, the Association announced a plan to 'Internationalize the Response' to airborne terrorism. *The Times* of London was the first newspaper to carry the story. In its 11 April edition, it told its readers that:

> The world's airlines are to press for the creation of an international force to take control of any future hijack and for hijackers to be tried by a new international court. Mr Rodney Wallis, Director of Security for the International Air Transport Association, said last night that he would press for the force to be introduced at a meeting of the International Civil Aviation Organization in June.

Evidence that the idea of an international force was supported by the UK government, came via its Foreign Secretary, who presented the idea, together with the IATA proposal for an internationally-based team to investigate incidents, to other European foreign ministers. In addition, the UK placed the proposals before ICAO, thus replicating the earlier IATA action. Although debate has moved both ideas forward, the intent of the original proposals has become somewhat diffused. This is always a danger within a United Nations body. The success of such a programme depends on the central organization initiating action just as the success of IATA's survey programme resulted primarily from the Association making the first move. ICAO has chosen to go the passive route: waiting for a government in need of assistance to approach them. There is perhaps room in the ICAO strategic action plan for the IATA approach to be considered as a *modus operandi* for the UN body.

International action following the Bosnia conflict, with a UN-initiated tribunal in the Hague trying persons indicted for war crimes, shows that the IATA proposal for such a court to try terrorists is more than feasible. Colonel Gadaffi has offered to release the two men indicted for the Lockerbie bombing to such a court.

IATA's role as an initiator of new thoughts seeking *safe, regular and economical* air transportation is key to the enhancement of aviation security. It must be used as the driving force for practical implementation of effective security management. Despite the ICAO strategic action plan, the potential for securing commercial aviation against the worst ravages of terrorism is more likely to stem from activity by the air carriers than from the efforts of governments.

ECAC

As already discussed, the power of the European Civil Aviation Conference (ECAC) exceeds that normally associated with regional organizations. They are able to use their collective voice in the larger ICAO forum to promote policies which, acting unilaterally, they may not have anticipated achieving. ECAC's strength comes from the largely common purposes and background similarities of its members. The Conference, when it meets on specialised subjects, is able to bring together small gatherings of experts from its member countries. They can draw on the fiscal resources and firm administrations of stable governments.

Acting independently of ICAO, ECAC can adopt procedures well in advance of those established by the UN body and indeed can usually draw on its member states' collective experience with new procedures when proposing or supporting the introduction of standards and recommended practices in the world forum.

ECAC's policies are developed within subdivisions of the Working Group on Security Problems. IATA, the International Federation of Airline Pilots Associations (IFALPA) and the ACI all send experts to the ECAC meetings, although there was early opposition by the UK's Department of Transport (DoT) to their participation.

The strange reluctance of the UK authorities to accept input by the professionals in the air transport industry to governmental development of regional security standards has never been satisfactorily explained.

The non-governmental organisations regularly participate in ICAO sessions and, as has been shown, one of them, IATA, was conceived by governments themselves at the 1944 Chicago Conference and charged with working in harness with ICAO. The DoT is isolated in holding its policy position, indeed several European governments include the security representative of the national air carrier in their delegations to ECAC. The DoT opposition may reflect their marked reluctance to having any person or group, other than themselves, being in a position to comment on international regulation and requirements to their political superior, the Minister of Aviation. A British airline participating under the IATA banner or briefed by the IATA secretariat would be able to do just this. The Association's pro-active policy in areas of aviation security, providing them with opportunities to meet directly with aviation ministers of all governments, may have marked it and its UK members for a DoT 'black ball'.

The combined output of the ECAC subgroups' work appears in the form of a Manual of Recommendations and Resolutions known as DOC. No. 30.. First authorised by the Twelfth Triennial Session of the ECAC which met in Strasbourg in 1985, DOC. No. 30 is worthy of study by any student of civil aviation security. Security began as a sub-section of the Facilitation Committee. It is worth noting that in ICAO also, security standards were first published as an integral part of its Facilitation Annex, Annex 9. Facilitation had long been the driving force of most major passenger service advances at the world forum. The two subjects, Facilitation (making things easier) and Security (adding more controls) were seen, once they separated, as being two opposing disciplines. The author of this paper, having had both responsibilities within IATA for almost a decade, saw them as complementary, neatly fitting under the overall mandate to promote *safe, regular and economical* air transport. However, after years of effective operation, IATA chose to separate the two responsibilities. ICAO, in contrast, elected to bring the two together once again, the latter recognising the value of the two subjects being managed in harness to the benefit of all users of the international air transport system.

The evolution of facilitation and security working in harness can be experienced every time a passenger passes a screening check point. When they were first introduced, security screening procedures meant passengers had to be physically searched and hand baggage rummaged by guards. By applying facilitation techniques, the physical frisking was replaced by magnetometers (metal detector archways) enabling the majority of passengers to walk through the screening process without pause or loss of dignity. X-rays allowed hand baggage to be inspected without the embarrassment of having one's belongings turned out for all to see. Facilitation does not have to be the enemy of security; the two disciplines *are* complimentary. ECAC recognized this and, while upgrading security in status, they maintained the two functions in harness, retitling the controlling body the Facilitation and Security Committee.

ECAC's ability to respond quickly to changing circumstances requiring an enhancement of security procedures was demonstrated by their early adoption of IATA's operating procedures for passenger and baggage reconciliation. These had been developed to maximise the security and customer service benefits of passenger and baggage matching, whether used in a manual or automated mode. For the latter method, IATA had developed specifications for baggage labels and boarding passes using a ten-digit bar code capable of being read by a laser reader. They brought supermarket stock control technology to the airlines enabling effective security control to be applied to baggage. The purpose was to prevent the carriage of unauthorised, unaccompanied bags. ECAC rationally adopted the airlines' policies, even incorporating IATA's diagrams into DOC. 30. The member states saw the airline association's approach as a cost-effective means of minimizing the threat posed by unaccompanied bags transporting improvised explosive devices. This type of collaboration, combining the technical and practical experience of the operators and the regulatory power of the civil aviation administrations, works to the benefit of all air travellers.

ECAC's inability to enforce their own policies does mean that decisions to implement them remains with the individual governments. Despite Lockerbie, passenger and baggage reconciliation procedures published in DOC. 30 in the late 1980s were not fully adopted by the UK until 1994.

ECAC uses its published recommendations to seek standardisation of programmes and procedures throughout the European region. Specifications governing high-tech detection equipment are provided. Published guidelines provide valuable data for use when reviewing potential technical purchases and when establishing maintenance schedules. These guidelines are used by member states when advising

Third World countries on security methodology. ECAC's interest in security standards at airports outside Europe stems from the simple truism that every departure of an aircraft from Europe to a Third World airport is matched by a return flight from the overseas location. There is little point safeguarding air transport operations outbound from European airports if the aircraft, their crews and passengers are to be left vulnerable on their return.

Some ECAC members, acting unilaterally and/or in harness, visit the developing world airports in their efforts to upgrade aviation security. These states consider they have a responsibility for their national air carrier operations wherever the airlines fly. They are aware of widely varying standards of security offered in different parts of the world. The importance of the above policy position was underlined in 1996 and again in 1997 when a British Airways aircraft, departing developing world airport, carried stowaways in the nose-wheel bay of the vehicles. If it is possible for would-be refugees to access an aircraft undetected, what of terrorists who could so easily plant an improvised explosive device in this very vulnerable position? The UK authorities could act unilaterally in an approach to the various countries in an endeavour to tighten airport security (the airline should also review its own standards) but ECAC's voice, speaking collectively for its member states, would carry greater weight. ECAC would enhance the safety of European commercial aviation operations if they were able to expand their mandate, giving themselves the power to seek responsive answers from any foreign state where security weaknesses have been identified. A variation on the mandate given to the IATA Director General by the Association's members could probably be obtained for the Secretary of ECAC if constructive debate were undertaken by the Directors of Civil Aviation who make up the Organisation's governing committee.[2] Alternatively, it is perhaps a role which the Transport Commissioner of the European Union could take on board. To date, the EU has shown a reluctance to become involved in aviation security matters but perhaps this is just a matter of time.

It can be seen that the international organisations work within limited parameters when seeking to enhance aviation security. Their primary role is one of policy development. ICAO provides the essential tools to enable standardised national programmes to be established worldwide, but is unable to ensure implementation of its rules. ECAC works within its region to provide speed and flexibility of response to meet the changing needs of civil aviation in its response to the evolution of terrorism. It also offers practical support to Third World countries of interest to European civil air operators but like ICAO, cannot enforce its own measures. IATA has pursued a pro-active role, firstly working to develop defences against acts of terrorism then to promote them through the intra-governmental bodies. IATA seeks to pre-empt such acts by physically working throughout the world to obtain implementation of the international security standards. However, like ICAO and ECAC, their role in respect of implementation is one of persuasion not enforcement.

Where does the ACI fit into this global picture?

ACI

The evolution of the ACI since its formation in 1991 has been dramatic. By the summer of 1997, its membership had reached 475 international airports and airport authorities running some 1200 airports in 152 countries and territories. The ACI sees its role as fostering co-operation among airport administrations and with other partners in world aviation. It has a similar goal to IATA in that it seeks to achieve *safe, secure, efficient* air transport operations *compatible with the environment.*

The ACI provides a forum for airport administrations to meet and discuss a wide range of mutually beneficial subjects. Today, the facilitation and security committees work in harness with those of IATA but it was not always this way. The collaborative effort was born out of a combative cycle of events in which the two bodies had fought a public, running battle in ICAO fora throughout the late 1970s and early 1980s. Government agencies were confused by the often conflicting positions taken by the commercial bodies and opportunities to maximise operational benefits were missed.

Recognizing that their respective members would frequently have opposing views but that such positions had to be reconciled and mutually agreed international procedures established, the ACI and IATA secretariats created joint working groups to debate operational needs and seek compromise positions to the benefit of both organizations and their customers. The first of the areas to be covered were Facilitation and Security. Today the ACI and IATA publish joint security guidelines seeking to maximise the opportunities resulting from airline and airport management co-operation. This co-operation was taken one step further in 1997 when the two organizations combined to host an ACI/IATA Aviation Security World Conference in Cairo. At the executive level, the two organizations are linked via the High-Level ACI/IATA Contact Committee whose members include the Directors General of both bodies.

The co-operative approach established in the 1980s has enabled joint positions to be developed and presented cohesively within ICAO, strengthening the potential for practical solutions to be adopted. The two commercial organizations are now better able to work towards achieving their common goals of *safe, secure, and efficient* security operations through the implementation of standard programmes around the world.

Different priorities remain within the two organizations. Their evolution and purpose of their operations, while both aimed at serving the flying public, are dissimilar in many respects. Airlines are international companies with services operating in a diverse range of countries with many different cultures, ethnic and economic backgrounds and management styles. Airline executives, if they are to be effective, must develop an understanding of the various environments in which their companies operate. They have to blend the various security operations demanded by a wide range of authorities into a programme acceptable to their own managements and governments whilst meeting the demands of the local authorities into whose airports their aircraft fly. In contrast, airports are static. Their managements, in the main, need only meet the requirements of a single government, albeit one which should be following standard ICAO policies. Unlike many airline managers, airport executives may well have had their experience confined to a single location or country. The ACI provides a forum which enables such managers to benefit from input by their counterparts in such contrasting locations as Heathrow and Chicago, Papeete and Lusaka. IATA and ACI, through their joint working groups seek to blend the combined airline/airport experiences into a harmonious approach.

In 1994, the ACI followed an earlier IATA initiative by creating a forum for airport (in the case of IATA, airline) and related business managements to meet, exchange information, develop markets and co-operate for their mutual benefit. The ACI package is the World Business Partners Programme.

FAA

The brief for this chapter was to discuss the role of the international organizations in enhancing aviation security. Even so it would be wrong not to mention, albeit in passing, one national (federal) civil aviation organization. The US Federal Aviation Administration (FAA) is a powerful, influential and generous agency offering many benefits to international civil aviation companies and authorities. Technical and training facilities are made available to foreign governments and aviation entities. Because of the size of US civil aviation operations, FAA rules and regulations frequently affect international carriers and airports in other hemispheres. However, because FAA rules are developed in a largely domestic environment and may be influenced by familial commercial concerns, regulations can differ from those in force elsewhere in the world.

An example of the above is the US policy on passenger and hand baggage screening. In a proposed rule change to the US Airport Security Programme (August 1997), the FAA reiterated that the responsibility for ensuring the integrity of the sterile area at an airport rests mainly with air carriers. In Europe and elsewhere, that responsibility normally lies directly with the airport or civil authority.

The USA has grandfather rights at ICAO where they are permanent members of the Council and thus are able to influence debate within the Organization. US air carriers are important members of IATA while US airport managements have powerful voices within the ACI. In this way, FAA policy can and does influence the development of international regulation over a broad spectrum however the latter sometimes falls short of or is at variance with the perceived needs of the US government. Where the US has sovereignty – that is, within its boundaries – federal rules apply and international carriers must conform with such regulations, but attempts to enforce US policies at overseas locations are sometimes made. This extra-territorial approach can result in acrimonious dispute which has to be resolved by bilateral discussion or perhaps in the multinational fora provided by the international organisations. A common, worldwide security programme is dependent upon harmonization of many policies and this can only be achieved through the international organizations.

Summary

This text has sought to show the role of the international aviation organisations in enhancing aviation security. The development of international conventions, standards, procedures and practises is the result of all the Organizations working in partnership. Their continued co-operation and co-ordination is essential for further, practical enhancement of aviation security.

NOTES

1. A special meeting of the ICAO Council was convened early in 1989 when several of the permanent Council members were replaced by their respective Ministers of Civil Aviation.
2. 'During and/or after actual incidents of air piracy, intervene as necessary with individual states … .where IATA involvement may result in a faster resolution of the situation.'

8

Aviation Security in the
United States

BRIAN M. JENKINS

Within days of the crash of TWA Flight 800, President Clinton created the White House Commission on Aviation Safety and Security, which was chaired by Vice President Gore. Such commissions have often been called upon in moments of national crisis and represent a unique policy-influence mechanism. They allow a president to be seen taking immediate action while buying time for reflection. Commissions are non-partisan, above the interests of competing government bureaucracies, and therefore objective. They combine recognized expertise, experience, and convey credibility. They represent and, since their reports are public, report to the people. And they can shake things up.

Political violence has often been the impetus for such commissions. Commissions were created to review the investigation into the assassination of President John F. Kennedy in 1963 to reflect upon the growing violence in the streets and the assassination of Martin Luther King and presidential candidate Robert F. Kennedy in 1968, to review the events that led to the shooting of student anti-war protesters by National Guardsmen in 1970, to examine the devastating terrorist bombing of the US Marine barracks in Beirut in 1983 and the Pentagon's preparedness for dealing with terrorism, and following the terrorist sabotage of Pan Am Flight 103 in 1988.

All such commissions involve a measure of political theater, especially in an election year, but in a tumultuous democracy where many important issues compete for attention and resources, tragedy and often theater are, regrettably, prerequisite to getting things done. This time was no different.

The composition of the Gore Commission itself reflected logic, bureaucratic and party politics, the need for credibility, and the desire for diversity. The 18 Commissioners included current government officials serving in the Department of Transportation, National Transportation Safety Board, Federal Bureau of Investigation, Central Intelligence Agency, Office of Management of the Budget, and the President's Council of Economic Advisors. Former government officials were also included for their expertise and to ensure bipartisanship. Also among the Commission members were future political appointees, members of the families of victims in the Pan Am 103 crash, trusted administration workhorses, and a handful of 'experts' selected from the academic community and private sector. Commission members were assisted by an superbly-led staff drawn from across government. Uncertain what brought down TWA 800 but certain that the crash of a Valujet airliner only weeks before was accidental, the White House Commission was charged with reviewing both aviation safety and security.

The Commission ultimately made 57 recommendations affecting four areas: safety, air traffic control, security, and response to aviation disasters. Some of the recommendations could be labeled as exhortation, some were goal-setting, many – especially in the security area – were specific and precise. Included in the mix were some bold assertions: The Commission proposed that aviation security be considered as a part of providing 'for the common defense', a constitutional imperative for the federal government; this would have important financial consequences. The Commission asserted that the accident rate, already low, could be cut by 80 per cent and that progress toward installing a new satellite-based air traffic control system could be significantly accelerated. The Commission urged that new explosives detection technology be deployed immediately with federal money, but that passengers themselves should ultimately bear the burden of increased security costs. Although it is hoped that its recommendations on safety and the modernization of the air traffic control system will have far-reaching effects in the coming years, the Commission's recommendations on security are producing the most immediate effects.

Not everyone would agree with the Commission's view that security needed to be improved. Security measures are disruptive and expensive. They ask 'Where's the threat?'. The absence of consensus on the nature and magnitude of the terrorist threat continues to be one of the principal obstacles to maintaining an effective aviation security program. The terrorist threat in the United States is real – witness the bombings of the World Trade Center, in Oklahoma City, Atlanta, and other plots discovered and thwarted by authorities – but it is diverse, amorphous, and difficult to depict in terms that allow precise calculation of security measures or that convince determined skeptics that such measures are even necessary. Terrorist events are always statistically rare. Unlike the United Kingdom or some other countries, the USA has not confronted a continuing terrorist campaign. Terrorists have not attacked commercial aviation there, although US airliners abroad often have been the target of terrorist attacks.

Dangerous adversaries are not confined to terrorists. Hijackings are still occasionally attempted in the USA, and its airports have been bombed. US airliners have unknowingly carried mail bombs in their holds. Bomb threats indicate continued interest in aviation as a target. Security screeners continue to intercept thousands of weapons, although we cannot count these as indicators of potential attack; however in 1987, a former airline employee smuggled a weapon on board a flight in California which he used to kill the pilot and co-pilot, bringing the plane down and killing all on board. We also must keep in mind that the threat is dynamic. Any perceived slackening of the security effort may encourage would-be adversaries to attempt an attack.

Still, the risk to individual citizens of dying in a terrorist incident of any type is infinitesimal, ignoring the broader social and political effects of terrorism. Intelligence about terrorism is usually imprecise; the noise level is high and inevitably there are numerous false alarms which further erode the credibility of warnings. Paradoxically, there is at the same time a tendency to overestimate the determination and capabilities of terrorist adversaries, dismally concluding that nothing can be done to stop them and that security that is less than perfect gives a false sense of confidence and wastes resources. Only when disasters occur do we lurch, sometimes blindly, toward security.

The Commission's initial focus on security measures does not mean that its members assumed that TWA 800 had been brought down by a bomb. More compelling was a terrorist plot discovered a year earlier in the Philippines to put bombs on board 12 US airliners in the Pacific. Ramzi Yousef, the alleged mastermind of this ambitious scheme and also one of those accused of involvement in the World Trade Center bombing, was on trial as the Commission began its deliberations, and was later convicted.

Commercial aviation has long been a favorite target of terrorists, who have viewed airliners as nationally-labeled containers of hostages in the case of hijackings, or victims in the case of sabotage. This set off a deadly contest between terrorists and security which has continued for the past 30 years with security gradually gaining. In the early 1970s, more than 30 per cent of international terrorist attacks were targeted against commercial aviation; it is less than 10 per cent today.

As discussed in my chapter on sabotage in this same volume, bombs remain the biggest threat. Terrorists have attempted to plant bombs on board airliners on more than 70 occasions that we know about. These have caused at least 15 crashes killing 1,732 persons. There are several more crashes where sabotage is suspected but not confirmed. These incidents conform to a disturbing terrorist trend toward large-scale indiscriminate violence.

Here, too, increased security appears to have had some effect. The 1970s saw 18 attempts to sabotage aircraft with eight crashes. The 1980s saw 13 attempts with six crashes. There have been fewer attempts in the 1990s with only one crash attributed to a terrorist bomb. Following the crash of Pan Am 103, the US Government invested heavily in research on explosives detection technology. As a result of this, and concurrent research abroad, there are now a variety of systems in various stages of development, production and deployment. No single explosives detection technology provides the desired level of confidence and efficiency, although at the time of the Commission's deliberations, only one device had been certified by the FAA. It will require a combination of technologies and procedures – a multilayered system – to arrive at an optimal solution. The only way to find out what combinations work best is to try them under actual operating conditions at airports throughout the country; test them aggressively, and see what works best. Recognizing that there is no 'silver bullet', the Commission recommended that the existing detection technology be deployed throughout US airports. Hopefully, three things will happen. We will learn which equipment and combinations of equipment work best; improvements will be made in the technology – the Commission also recommended a joint government/industry program to continue research – and by creating a demand for increased production, the costs per machine will come down. It is an experiment with no downside.

Some combinations will prove highly effective, some undoubtedly less so, but all airports will reap some security benefit. No airport's security will be less.

The Commission also recommended the implementation of full passenger bag-match to ensure that terrorists cannot check-in a suitcase with a bomb and then not board the flight. This is now done on international flights. Matching baggage with passengers poses no great technical difficulty. Problems arise, and airline resistance grows when passengers and bags transfer from one flight to another. Passengers may make the second flight while their bags do not, which poses less of a threat because passengers do not control or even necessarily know whether their suitcase has made the flight. Of greater concern are when bags are transferred from one flight to another but passengers fail to board the second flight and the loaded bag must then be located and pulled. The airlines claim this happens often enough to cause numerous delays and, since US airlines operate on a hub system, the disruption would be significant. Critics claim that the industry has exaggerated both the frequency and the resulting disruption.

The Commission compromised by recommending that US airlines by the end of 1997 have a system in place to match all baggage but pull transferred bags only when that bag has *not* gone through an explosives detection device at the first airport and belongs to a passenger selected by the passenger profiling system, both of which could be indicated on the bar code. In other words, once inspected, a bag could travel through the system even unaccompanied; so could an inspected bag if it belonged to a passenger not selected by the profile.

The deployment of explosives detection machines and additional bomb-sniffing dog teams in addition to bag matching are two components of the Commission's plan to keep bombs off airliners. The third and most controversial component is passenger profiling. Until we have the technology and procedures in place to ensure that no passenger, no carry-on, or checked baggage might carry or contain explosives, it will remain necessary to select some passengers or their luggage for more detailed inspection. That requires profiling, something a number of non-US airports and carriers have been doing for some time. But any form of selection for additional scrutiny is contentious in a society as ethnically diverse as America's, where civil liberties are constitutionally guaranteed and citizens are exquisitely sensitive to any form of discrimination.

Americans would prefer their security to be democratic and passive; that is, equally applied to everyone, and reactive only to behavior indicating criminal intent – such as attempting to smuggle a gun on board – rather than attempting to identify in advance the most likely smuggler. Criteria based on ethnic identity, national origin, gender, and religion are all out of bounds to civil libertarians. Nor should profiling provide airlines with access to personal information about travelers, including their criminal record if they have one.

Arab-Americans, who have been subject to suspicion and in some cases mistreatment following terrorist incidents that were correctly or incorrectly blamed on Middle Eastern groups, have expressed particular concern. In public testimony before the Commission, their spokespersons described several cases of embarrassing treatment based on ethnic discrimination, although curiously two of the three examples they chose involved El Al and the third Lufthansa.

There has been a great deal of misunderstanding about the profiling measure, some of it deliberate. In fact, the model automated profiling system, which is being developed by North West Airlines, is based not on some secret terrorist profile but primarily on how much the airline already knows about the boarding passenger – or does not know. Often the passenger will not even know if he has been singled out by the profile; his checked bag will merely be scrutinized more closely. To meet civil libertarian concerns and increase security, the Commission recommended that in addition to the 'selectees' identified by the system, a number of randomly selected passengers will be added. This would ensure that 'selectees' are not automatically treated as suspects and it will increase the risks to terrorists who think they can beat the profile.

These, in my view, are interim measures, although nearly a year and a half later, they are yet to be fully implemented. The need for profiling and baggage match will decline as reliable explosive detection technology is deployed throughout all airports. The need to pull any bags at a hub would be eliminated by rigorous inspection of all selected passengers at the first emplanement. As more EDS machines are deployed, the number of uninspected bags will decline and the protocol for pulling bags can be stiffened with little disruption of airline schedules, but that may take several more years. Not surprisingly, the industry agreed to this initial mild requirement and endorsed the Commission's recommendations.

Unfortunately, the weak point continues to be the people hired to man the security posts and operate the security systems. Rather than devote more money to improving the quality of security personnel, the industry would prefer a technological solution devoid of any need for human interpretation or intervention. Security failures often occur not because machines do not work but because humans fail. Yet while airlines lament the low quality of the people contracted to man the checkpoints, contracts to security providers are still negotiated primarily on the basis of cost. The result is a minimum wage workforce with all the attendant problems of motivation, education, receptiveness to training, reliability and high turnover.

A more professional security force is required. The Commission tried to tackle this by recommending FAA certification of companies that provide passenger and luggage security as a means of thereby imposing upon them some minimum standards for training. We should go further. Through federal certification of security companies, higher standards, improved basic training, and advanced individual training, we should move toward the creation of an air security profession. While remaining in the private sector, the FAA can establish standards, training requirements, certification of individuals, and even a common rank structure that would allow a qualified individual to move from company to company at roughly the same pay grade. A point system can be established to recognize the collective training and experience of the personnel in the competition for contracts. Aggressive testing by the FAA and intercompany security 'tournaments' could also lead to performance scorecards.

Numerous eye witnesses have testified that they saw a streak of light heading toward Flight 800 before it exploded, raising the possibility that the airplane had been hit by a missile. Although investigators thus far have found no physical evidence of a missile, surface-to-air missiles in the hands of terrorists do pose a growing threat to commercial aviation.

Shoulder-fired, heat-seeking surface-to-air missiles (SAMs) are mass produced, highly portable, easy to use, hard to detect and have proved effective even against low-flying combat aircraft. Several hundred thousand of these weapons are currently in the arsenals of nearly 100 countries and their population is growing as new, more sophisticated versions are deployed; 25 guerrilla armies or terrorist organizations are believed to possess them, a number that has increased over the past two decades. During that time there have been approximately 40 missile attacks on civilian aircraft causing more than 700 deaths, although no attacks have occurred outside of conflict zones, no US commercial airliners have been shot down by missiles, and, outside of military arsenals, no weapons have been found in the USA. Countermeasures are available but are disruptive and costly, thus raising the question (as in virtually all security measures against terrorism) of whether the reduction in risk justifies the cost and consequences, especially when the danger is real but remote. The Commission adopted a conservative posture, calling for an inter-agency task force to review the threat and develop appropriate plans. At the same time it urged that the USA seek international co-operation to keep surface-to-air missiles out of terrorists' hands.

How much security is enough? In dealing with often spectacular but statistically rare terrorist events, that question is difficult to answer. Cost-benefit analysis does not help much here and can be counterproductive. The Commission recommended that while cost-benefit analysis can enlighten the decision-making process, cost alone should not become 'dispositive' in deciding safety or security issues.

Despite the threat of terrorism, airline travel is extremely safe. The risk of death to individual passengers from any cause is minuscule, making it difficult to argue for any security measure on the grounds that it will save lives. The probability of dying in an automobile accident is one in 5,000; of being murdered, one in 12,000; of being killed by a terrorist, one in millions. The National Academy of Sciences calculated the chance of an airline passengers' bag containing a bomb at one in 1.2 billion. If casualties were the sole criterion, cost-benefit analysis might even be used perversely to justify reducing safety expenditures even at the risk of a greater number of accidents, so long as airline travel remained significantly safer than other modes of transportation on a passenger-mile basis. But casualties are not the only measure. Successful terrorist attacks create widespread alarm, provoke government crises, erode citizens' faith in their institutions, and impose other 'costs' on society that are important but difficult to quantify. Moreover, security measures have both a preventive and a deterrent function. Had no security measures been imposed, almost certainly some terrorist attacks would have occurred. The author also suspects that good security would survive a market test; that is, passengers would choose to travel on an airline with good security over one with no security in order to save a few dollars.

The security measures recommended by the Commission will cost billions of dollars over the long run. The White House Commission left the details of who will pay and how to the National Civil Aviation Review Commission created by Congress for expressly that purpose in late 1996, but it did offer suggestions and advance some general principles. The first proposition offered by the Commission was that a terrorist attack on any US airliner was not an attack on the airline or the industry but an attack on all Americans, and therefore a matter of national security.

Arguing that protecting aviation is part of government's responsibility 'to provide for the common defense', as dictated by the Commission, the Commission recommended that Congress appropriate funds to pay for the initial package of security recommendations and approve a continued federal contribution to future security costs going forward. This was a bold assertion but Congress agreed and promptly approved several hundred millions to fund the Commission's initial recommendations. In its Final Report, the White House Commission recommended continued funding at the level of $100 million a year for the next five years. The money is to be used primarily for capital investment, specifically the deployment of additional explosives detection devices.

The reality of terrorism precludes the government from assuming the entire security burden. Terrorists can attack anything, anywhere, anytime. The government cannot protect everything, everywhere, all the time. The burden of security against terrorism must be shared by national and local government, by the public and private sector, and by the flying public. The Commission advanced the proposition that users pay. That would put the ultimate burden on the flying passenger. By whatever means the money is collected, passengers will pay for security. With a half billion emplanements a year in the USA, security costs per passenger are modest – one to a few dollars per flight – depending on what one includes in the calculations.

This author would go a step further than the White House Commission and remove the task of security from the airlines (and their bottom line considerations) by creating a series of non-profit public trusts, funded by a set fee per ticket, independently managed but government regulated, and dedicated exclusively to the function of security.

Aviation security is not a product of threat analysis that leads to easy agreement on appropriate countermeasures. It is a contentious issue that arouses numerous competing interests – advocates of greater security, major airlines, regional carriers, air couriers and air freight forwarders, airports, aircraft manufacturers, airline crews, the security industry, law enforcement agencies, government bureaucracies, Congress, foes of federal regulation, civil libertarians. Each has its own agenda.

Reasonable persons may disagree as members of the Commission did. There was debate, sometimes intense although nothing like the 'bitter behind closed doors disputes' mentioned in some news media accounts. One of the commissioners, whose husband had been killed in the bombing of Pan Am 103, disagreed with the Commission's final report. In her view, the Commission should have demanded more stringent security measures, more federal money to fund them, and set strict deadlines for their implementation. As the Commission's lone dissenter, her views received widespread publicity.

The Commission's recommendations received mixed reviews. Some criticized the Commission for not going far enough while others criticized it for going too far. One critic described its report as 'toothless'. As evidence of 'toothless' language, the first critic cited the Commission's recommendation that the 'Postal Service should advise customers that all packages weighing over 16 ounces [454g] will be subject to examination for explosives and other threat objects in order to be moved by air'. This, he suggested, meant that such packages *may* be examined, not that they *will* be, which in his view, would have been the preferred language. As a matter of fact, the United States Postal Service successfully objected to this measure, arguing that implementation would impede the ability of the Postal Service to compete with other companies, require new equipment, cause extensive delay of the mail, and violate the sanctity and privacy of the mail and US Constitution-guaranteed protection against warrantless search. Others protested that the Commission's recommendations and the resulting legislation were 'based upon emotion rather than reason'.

A commission can only recommend. Its mandate provides no power beyond persuasion. Its members were mindful that many of the measures recommended by previous commissions and task forces were delayed, diluted, and remain unenforced. Some slippage may be inevitable in a democratic process, and many obstacles stood in the way: lack of consensus on the threat, the highly competitive airline industry's resistance to spending money or increasing charges to passengers, effective lobbying at the White House and in Congress, efforts to achieve a balanced federal budget, a slow, often cumbersome rule-making process, and fleeting focus as other issues commanded immediate attention. Nonetheless, progress has been made.

Aviation security has been recognized as a major element in America's strategy against terrorism. Federal funding for aviation security was increased, although not at the sustained $100 million a year recommended by the Commission. New explosives detection technology supplemented by canine explosives detection teams are being deployed, and some airports – notably at the new Terminal 1 at New York's JFK, which has deployed an array of different detection technologies to inspect all bags – detection technologies are being improved.

An automated passenger profiling system known as Computer-Assisted Passenger Screening or CAPS is being implemented. An FAA rule on profiling is targeted for completion in 1998, but it is anticipated that all major carriers will have phased in CAPS before federal regulation mandates its use as the method of determining which passengers' bags must be subjected to additional security measures such as bag matching or screening with explosives detection systems. The expansion of bag-passenger match should accompany the implementation of CAPS, although this is something to watch.

One, of course, would like to have seen less politics, less resistance, more secure funding, faster progress in achieving the security goals laid out by the Commission. Fortunately, we have not yet suffered another airline tragedy that would accelerate the process.

9

Aviation Security Before and After Lockerbie

OMAR MALIK

The destruction of Pan Am 103 transformed British attitudes to aviation security. It was an act of wanton murder, and one which most people had believed unthinkable and the experts had believed unlikely. The event occurred four days before Christmas, adding poignancy to horror. Three hundred tons of wreckage and fuel fell on the peaceful Scottish town of Lockerbie. The fireball reached 10,000 feet. 43 British subjects, 11 of whom were residents of Lockerbie, were amongst the 270 innocent people who died. The B747 had taken off from Britain's premier airport, London Heathrow. It was destroyed in British airspace and crashed on British territory. The aircraft belonged to the national airline of Great Britain's closest ally, the USA. There was speculation that the loss was the product of deficient security at Heathrow. All these factors combined to capture close media, public and official attention. Aviation security activity in Great Britain underwent a transformation.

There had been two reasons for its previously pedestrian progress. First, the threat to aviation was viewed as meriting steady, but not urgent, countermeasures. In the preceding twenty years there had been only four serious terrorist attacks on British aircraft. Each had had a specific purpose: the release of a terrorist from custody. The most recent had been 14 years earlier, in 1974. The low priority accorded by HMG to the subject was reflected in its low allocation of resources to the Department of Transport's (DoT) aviation security operation, which had seven (sometimes less) advisers.[1] Second, HMG steadfastly refused to contribute to industry's costs, conveniently overlooking the fact that it, HMG, was the terrorists' true target and the industry only the unfortunate victim. Understandably, industry resented and resisted the continually increasing burden. Thus neither HMG nor industry were wholehearted in their pursuit of the highest practicable standards.

The destruction of Pan Am 103 changed HMG's attitude to the urgency of aviation security, but not to the extent of accepting responsibility to contribute to its costs. This conceptual flaw remains, and continues to inhibit the progress of British aviation security.

The Advent of International Terrorist Attacks on Aviation

Aircraft have been attacked by opponents of governments since 1931. However, it was not until 1968 that serial attacks on aviation were adopted as a terrorist tactic. In 1967, Israel had massively defeated Arab conventional forces; it had not been seriously affected by the Palestinians' earlier pinprick fedayeen attacks. The Palestinians had a desperate need for a different methodology. It is clear that their adoption of the new tactic was thoughtful.

It was intended to spread fear: 'We think that killing one Jew far from the field of battle is more effective than killing a hundred Jews on the field of battle because it attracts more attention,' (Habash).[2]

It was intended to do economic damage to Israel: '(Dr Habash) hoped that by hijacking and shooting up El Al's fleet of seven B-707's he could significantly reduce the major contribution the airline made to Israel's foreign currency reserves.'[3]

It was intended to be a tactic of Marxism-Leninism: 'We act heroically in a cowardly world to prove that the enemy is not invincible. We act "violently" in order to blow the wax out of the ears of the deaf Western liberals and to remove the straws that block their vision. We act as revolutionaries to inspire the masses and to trigger off the revolutionary upheaval in an era of counter revolution.' (Words of an unnamed comrade.)[4]

It was intended to damage the state of Israel: 'To Dr Habash, El Al was the symbol of Israel abroad, the flag-carrier which flaunted the permanence of a state which the Arabs refused to recognise.'[5]

It was intended also to damage Israel's supporters: 'The non-Israeli passengers were on their way to Israel. Since we have no control over the land that was stolen from us and called Israel, it is right that whoever goes to Israel should ask for our permission... And we will continue our present strategy. It's a smart one, you see, would you really want to fly El Al?' (Habash).[6]

From 1968 to 1970, the Palestinians had had a series of tactical successes. Initially they targeted El Al. With their first attack (22 July 1968), the hijack of an El Al B-707 to Algiers, they coerced Israel to release prisoners. Soon (29 August 1969) they targeted Israel's closest ally, the USA, hijacking a TWA B-707, flying it over Haifa and Tel-Aviv before landing in Damascus and coercing Israel to release more prisoners. They achieved their greatest *coup* in September 1970. In the Dawsons Field extravaganza, they hijacked and destroyed four aircraft, including the first British victim, a BOAC VC-10, and including a PanAm B-747 too large to land at Dawsons Field which was blown up at Cairo. For two years, the Palestinian operations, most of which were conducted by the PFLP, had been targeted rationally and, with the exception of the mid-air destruction of a Swissair Coronado and the attempted destruction of an Austrian Caravelle by the PFLP-GC (21 February 1970), had achieved considerable success with minimal bloodshed. However their greatest tactical triumph was also the first in a series of strategic disasters.

The integrity of Jordan and the throne of King Hussein had already been threatened by the presence of the Palestinian commandos. Dawsons Field marked a major departure from their customary activity of cross-border attacks on Israel. It involved the use of the Jordanian territory as a base for an international terrorist operation which targeted, amongst others, Great Britain and the USA, countries with whom Jordan enjoyed good relations. King Hussein had little choice but to reclaim the autonomy of his country. The Palestinians were driven out. Most went to the Lebanon. The disaster they soon brought upon that most democratic of Middle Eastern countries was a telling vindication of King Hussein's action.

The PLO policy of supposed political unity accompanied by military autonomy for its constituent factions was a complete nonsense. Disparate Palestinian and Middle Eastern groups took to attacking aviation targets. The tactic ceased to be a tool of Palestinian political strategy. At the same time, Israel protected El Al with stringent and effective security, a straightforward task for a small airline with a loyal customer base. Thus the aviation terrorists had more success targeting other countries, notably the USA. Control was steadily taken over by state-sponsors – by Libya, Syria, Iran and Iraq – as their price of accommodating the terrorist groups of Abu Nidal, Ahmed Jibril and others. By December 1988, international terrorist attacks on aviation had evolved into a tactic of state policy, an act of war in all but name. The terrorist groups that mounted the attacks provided a thin veneer of deniability with which their state masters cloaked their state murders. America had earned the enmity of Syria and the Arab world by its support of Israel. It had attracted the animosity of the Shiites by its intervention in Lebanon, of the Ayatollahs by its association with the Shah, of Gadaffi by bombing Libya. Then in July 1988, by dreadful accident, the *USS Vincennes* shot down an Iranian Airbus in the Gulf.

All the evidence suggests that the destruction of Pan Am 103 was instigated by one or more of these terrorist states.[7] No sponsor has dared claim 'credit', rightly fearful of richly merited retribution. The perpetrators' sole gain, by the murder of 270 innocents, was solipsistic, their own satisfaction and, with that, an ineradicable stain upon themselves.

Assessment of the Threat

Threat assessment is an advanced art. Like any art it can be improved, but not replaced, by science. The threat assessor must gauge, for each group of possible attackers, its attack potential – its capability (resources, expertise) to make an attack; and its attack probability – the likelihood that it will decide to mount an attack. The assessment must be made for targets both general and specific. Attack Probability is the command decision. It is normally not made by the terrorists but by their controllers, the attack instigators. The key factors are the instigators' criteria of success and their prediction of the probability of the attack meeting these criteria. In addition to the more general objectives articulated by Habash and others, the coerced release of prisoners, extortion, and publicity were the most common success criteria for attacks on aviation (1968–88). Early aviation terrorists achieved resounding successes in the achievement of all of them.

If it is accepted that the overwhelming factor in the motivation of attacks is the probability of achieving success, then it follows that the key to discouraging attacks is the denial of success. Great Britain learned this lesson much more quickly than most. HMG demonstrated its resolute stance on several occasions: Spaghetti House siege, 1975; Balcombe Street siege, 1975; Iranian Embassy siege, 1980. The last two of these and the successful Mogadishu rescue in 1977, served to broadcast the capabilities of the SAS the world over. Thus terrorist groups were aware that Britain had a policy of no concessions to terrorists, a Prime Minister, Margaret Thatcher, of indeflectable resolution, and Special Forces with formidable skills.

With hindsight, the 1988 threat assessment can be seen to have been substantially accurate. There were good grounds for believing that British aviation was not a prime terrorist target. Britain's most active terrorist group, PIRA, clearly appreciated that the destruction of civil aircraft would be seriously counterproductive to its political aims. Further, HMG's consistent condemnation of Israel's excesses saved Britain to some degree from the hostility of the most virulent Middle Eastern terrorist groups, although the possible use of Britain as a battleground was understood. Therefore, aviation security was not seen to merit high government priority and was allocated commensurately modest resources. With the same hindsight it could also be submitted that greater expenditure on the administration and inspection of aviation security by HMG might have prevented the loss of PanAm 103. This overlooks the inability of governments to resolve the issue of host-state responsibility. More important, it distracts from the fundamental fact that the existing US security system, had it been enforced by PanAm or the FAA, would have saved the 270 lives at Lockerbie.

The Fatal Accident Inquiry

The Fatal Accident Inquiry, a legal procedure required under Scottish law, was conducted by the Sheriff Principal, John S. Mowat QC. Unlike many legal processes following aircraft accidents, this enquiry is thought by the well-informed to have reached substantially accurate conclusions.[8] The bomb that destroyed Pan Am 103 on 21 December 1988 was concealed in a Toshiba radio-cassette player placed in a Samsonite suitcase. The suitcase was transferred to Pan Am 103 from Pan Am 103A at Heathrow. It was probably transferred to Pan Am 103A from another airline at Frankfurt. Close reading of the anodyne prose of the Sheriff's Determination and of the blunter wording of the US Report of the President's Commission reveals a horror story.

- On 18 November 1988 the FAA had issued a bulletin describing a Toshiba radio cassette-player which had been rigged as a bomb. It was equipped with a barometric device, suggesting that an aircraft might be the target. The bulletin cautioned that the device would be very difficult to detect via normal x-ray inspection.

- A key US rule 'prohibited any carrier from transporting baggage that was not either accompanied by a passenger or physically inspected.'[9]
- There was no positive passenger-baggage reconciliation procedure at Frankfurt.[10]
- The suitcase was not identified as an unaccompanied bag at Frankfurt.
- The suitcase was x-rayed, to a doubtful standard, at Frankfurt. It was not searched.
- There was no positive passenger- baggage reconciliation at Heathrow in relation to bags transferred from Flight 103A to Flight 103.
- The suitcase was not identified as an unaccompanied bag at Heathrow. Therefore:
- The suitcase was not x-rayed or searched at Heathrow.

Any one of these security measures, correctly applied, should have averted the loss of Pan Am 103. Nor is the above list exhaustive. Although it was not known where the Toshiba bomb was to have been used, the most elementary response to its discovery in Germany should have been to ensure meticulous adherence to security procedures at Germany's main international airport, Frankfurt.

The last three security measures relate to Heathrow and raise the question of the adequacy of the British security regime. The Determination did find that the DoT's enactments did not provide reasonable protection against an undetected unaccompanied bag being transferred to Flight 103. However it also found that 'Pan American knew that there were UK requirements that were binding on them but that they paid scant regard to them on the basis that the (US) rules were likely to be more stringent and that compliance with the latter would involve compliance with the former.'[11] The existing US rules would have prevented the loss, if they had been strictly enforced.

There was never any question of the British authorities enforcing the American rules. The delicate matter of host-state responsibility posed problems which were insuperable even to the closest of allies. Demarcation dictated that each country inspected and enforced its own rules only. US attempts to inspect British security were rebuffed on the grounds of infringement of national sovereignty. This is not relevant to the loss of Pan Am 103. The FAA had failed to enforce its own rules at Frankfurt. What is relevant is that demarcation difficulties, if not carefully addressed, translate into gaping holes in security.

In one matter, the handling of the Toshiba warning, the Sheriff let the DoT off lightly.[12] On 17 November 1988 the DoT received its first information on the discovery in Germany of a Toshiba radio-cassette player used to conceal an Improvised Explosive Device (IED), probably for an attack on an aircraft. On 8 December, the DoT received colour photographs. For various reasons the DoT did not circulate the photographs until after Christmas – Pan Am 103 having been bombed on 21 December. In explaining the delay, the DoT stated that '(it) was frustrated by the delay (in the copying of) the photographs but also by lack of any assessment of the area of threat from the security services'.[13] Thus a detailed warning, which should have been treated with urgency, was not. This tardiness, and the failure of co-ordination by two government departments, reveals a fundamental flaw in the organisation of security in Great Britain: the absence of a point of overall command, and an overall commander. It is not clear that this flaw has been corrected.

British Aviation Security at the Time of Lockerbie

For ease of comparison, the same simple framework is used to assess British aviation security in 1988 and, later in this paper, in 1998.[14]

There is an important perspective to the discussion of the weaknesses in British aviation security at the time of Lockerbie. It was the assessment of the British Airline Pilots Association that British aviation security standards were amongst the highest in the world. This assessment was a distillate of the experience of 4620 airline pilots and of worldwide airline operation.

The political direction suffered from three conceptual flaws:

- The direction was not holistic. There was no strategy.
- The command structure was, in executive terms, arguably non-existent. Command was diffused amongst the organisations involved. The various government departments and agencies were co-ordinated, presumably by a Cabinet Committee. However no single person had overall command, as evidenced by the dilatory handling of the Toshiba warning. Nor had the DoT established a

dominant relationship over the industry.
- HMG made no real contribution to the industry's costs of security, although it continually increased its demands. Thus the two key parties did not work effectively in partnership but in a continuous state of confrontation, with neither establishing long-term ascendancy.

The administrative system was also flawed.

- The DoT was under-resourced. The establishment of advisers was seriously inadequate.
- The DoT advisers were of modest rank. They therefore commanded limited respect in the industry.
- The DoT devoted its limited resources to writing policy; that is, drafting the enactments which defined aviation security standards.
- The DoT advisers lacked expertise in airline operations.
- The enactments were often ineptly worded; for example, '(airlines) should reasonably satisfy themselves'. They were therefore both capable of many interpretations; understandably, industry generally chose the most convenient.
- Most enactments had advisory rather than statutory status. Advice is not enforceable. Many airlines did not feel bound to follow advice.
- Statutory enactments, by reason of their inept wording, were an inadequate base for successful prosecution. They were probably unenforceable.
- The DoT advisers, by reason of their small number, were unable to carry out a meaningful programme of inspection. They were thus supposedly unaware of the standards of security achieved in practice.
- Had the DoT advisers been cognisant of the widespread non-compliance with DoT enactments, it is not clear what action they could successfully have taken.

Thus the administrative system was chronically under-resourced for anything other than slow, piecemeal progress. Enactments were sometimes flawed and compliance was often discretionary. The system achieved patchy results.

The standards themselves had grave weaknesses. The most serious were:

- The contemporary system of passenger-baggage reconciliation, the 'bedrock' of security, was badly flawed. This was highlighted by the Sheriff Principal in his Determination.[15] He emphasised the difference between 'positive' and 'negative' passenger-baggage reconciliation. 'Positive' involves a positive check that both passenger and bag are on the aircraft. 'Negative' reconciliation means that a bag is offloaded only when the passenger is known to be missing. At the time there were many avenues by which a passenger could go missing without his absence being known or detected. Negative reconciliation was the normal British practice.
- The screening methods which were applied to known unaccompanied hold bags were rudimentary.
- Reconciliation covered only hold baggage. It was not extended to cabin baggage. Thus when a passenger left the aeroplane there was no check that he had not left an explosive device or other prohibited article in the passenger cabin.
- The probity of staff with airside passes was not established, it was assumed. Given the large number of Irish and immigrant workers at British airports, potential PIRA or Palestinian terrorist sympathisers, this assumption was ill-founded. This problem was greatest at Heathrow, the size of which magnified the problem and where a significant number of new immigrants were employed.
- The security of cargo, and of most aircraft supplies, was assumed rather than assured.
- There were unaddressed gaps in security. One, potentially disastrous, was revealed by the loss of Pan Am 103. At the time, the threat was assessed correctly as less for British airlines than for those of the USA. More stringent procedures therefore applied to the latter. They were directed at protecting the target, the aircraft, and thus at intercepting prohibited articles *en route* to it. Procedures did not adequately cover the contingency of such articles being mis-routed or re-routed to an aircraft under lower threat, and therefore not protected by the same stringent procedures. BALPA was greatly concerned that, had Pan Am 103 been over-booked, delayed or cancelled, its baggage might well have been transferred and loaded on to a British aircraft without detection of the explosive device. These concerns were immediately telephoned to the DoT who addressed the issue with urgency.

Finally, aviation's long tradition of safety consciousness had not, in 1988, been extended to *security consciousness and commitment.* Career prospects of middle and junior airline managers depended upon the punctual departure of aircraft. Given the remoteness of the probability of a terrorist attack on any specific flight, many of them adjusted their priorities accordingly. Responsibility for these attitudes rested not with such managers, but with the senior managers of the airline who determined the corporate culture. An interesting example of this was reported to BALPA. A senior British Airways Captain believed that an aircraft dispatcher had deliberately given him a falsified report in order to avoid a security delay. The Captain submitted a formal report to the Head of Security whose attempts to remedy the situation foundered in a bog of bureaucracy. Therefore Sir Colin Marshall, the Chief Executive, was asked to put his own signature to an instruction to staff, affirming the primacy of security procedures. This he did. Staff then felt less vulnerable and attitudes to security improved markedly. Staff attitudes to security are as important as security regulations and procedures. Regulations and procedures are the building blocks of security; personnel attitudes are the cement – or the sand – which holds the blocks together. Developing the right corporate culture starts not with airline senior management but with HMG. Both before and after 1988 the relationship between HMG and industry has been, to a greater or lesser degree, confrontational.

The security of British aircraft overseas is a separate and much more difficult problem, because it impacts on the sovereignty of other nations. At an overseas airport it is unavoidable that much of the security (such as airport access, armed guards and policing) is in the hands of the host-state. However other aspects (passenger screening, baggage screening and handling) are often the exclusive preserve of local police or security agencies. In theory the host-state provides security which meets the standards of ICAO. In practice standards are a patchwork of inconsistency. Neither ICAO nor ECAC (the European body which deliberates aviation security) have authority over their member states. They have no effective mechanism for monitoring achieved standards, let alone enforcing them. Thus the degree of adherence to ICAO Standards, supposedly mandatory, and ICAO and ECAC Recommendations (advisory) is entirely a matter for each individual state to decide. Moreover all enactments have to be approved by the international community; consequently their content is primarily

a palliative to national psyches; the advancement of security comes a
poor second.

A passage from the British Airline Pilots Association Submission to
the Select Committee illustrates the realities of overseas security in
1988:[16]

> Security Overseas is generally flawed and in places, non-existent.
> The problems in obtaining acceptable standards are not to be
> under-estimated. As an example, Paris (Charles de Gaulle) has
> been the source of complaints from pilots for a matter of years;
> the Association and British Airways have joined in raising the
> issue at NASC; the Department of Transport has sought the
> assistance of the Foreign Office; the Embassy in Paris has pursued
> the matter. No improvements are evident, and this with France,
> our neighbour and fellow-member of the EEC. Problems are
> compounded in the Third World, where neither requisite funds
> nor expertise are available.

The Impact of Lockerbie

A fundamental difficulty which faces those who make threat
assessments is that the past is the basis for their prediction of the future.
The less their assessment is founded upon past experience or upon
reliable information, the less conviction it is likely to carry. A terrorist
with hostile intent to a target is limited in his selection of victim only by
his imagination.[17] Prior to Lockerbie, BALPA was probably the
organisation most active in Great Britain in pursuit of higher standards
of aviation security, although not because it differed with HMG's threat
assessment, nor because it claimed prescience on terrorist victim
selection. It was simply more aware of the widespread weaknesses in
aviation security than any other organisation; it considered that there
were many easy avenues open to a serious attacker. It knew that any
attack on a British aircraft would endanger its members. BALPA's
priority is the well-being of its members; an airline's priority is its
commercial survival; the DoT's priority is at the behest of the Secretary
of State, who has to juggle competing political pressures. Therefore
BALPA's endeavours to speed progress attracted opposition from
industry and little support from the DoT. The endeavours faced the
substantial counter-argument that there had been no serious attack on a

British aircraft for 14 years and that the threat was not high. Thus airlines felt that they were being asked to spend £100m's to try to prevent something that was not going to happen anyway. One airline pointed out that such sums would save more lives if spent on aviation safety instead of aviation security.

The attack on Pan Am 103 did not invalidate the threat assessment, nor did it invalidate the positions of the DoT or industry. It did change them. The fact of the attack raised the threat assessment to reflect the proven activity and capability of a terrorist group, and its encouragement by 'success'. It also changed the priorities of DoT and industry. Both, in the long run, are responsive to public opinion, respectively the electorate and the market. It was perceived that public opinion had been swung by the atrocity to demand measures to prevent a repetition. It was in response to that demand that aviation security in Great Britain was revitalised. The full mechanism of government moved into action. Parliament gave attention to the subject. A Select Committee conducted an investigation. The Secretary of State ordered a review. An Act was passed by Parliament. Many improvements followed.

For five years, 1988–93, aviation security in Great Britain was re-energised. Then, inevitably, the momentum imparted by Lockerbie was lost. There were three main reasons. First, during a period of Treasury inroads into government spending, TRANSEC (see below) had been established and had expanded. Second, the threat was thought to have diminished. The Gulf confrontation (1990–91) had passed without serious terrorist activity, successful pre-emptive action having been taken against Iraqi 'diplomat' controllers. The Gulf War had demonstrated the accuracy of US Cruise missiles and laser-guided bombs, and diminished state-sponsors' comfortable feelings of their own invulnerability. Third, by 1993 TRANSEC had achieved most of the advances that were readily achievable and was facing a future of diminishing returns. Therefore, in 1993, the Treasury, having been held off for five years, demanded its piece of flesh. Thus in the ten years that have followed Lockerbie, two distinct periods can be distinguished in aviation security activity in Great Britain: the re-energisation years 1988–93, and the reorganisation years 1993–98.

The Department of Transport

In December 1988, the Secretary of State for Transport was Paul Channon. Although Lockerbie brought about his resignation, largely because of an ill-received holiday soon after the event, he was highly regarded by both sides of the House and by many involved in aviation security. He appeared at the National Aviation Security Committee (NASC) and sought submissions from all the organisations involved. These and the Report of the Transport Committee (see below) were taken into account by the DoT in undertaking the wide-ranging review of aviation security which Paul Channon initiated.

The most important reflection of the new priority accorded by HMG to aviation security was the new department, TRANSEC (Transport Security), established within the DoT. TRANSEC was given responsibility for Aviation, Maritime and Tunnel security. Its establishment grew to 135 (1992/93), which size was an indication of the impossible task that the DoT's seven advisers had faced. The direction and management of TRANSEC was placed in capable hands. All its activities gained momentum. More importantly, they were extended into the areas of inspecting, testing and auditing. Thus, for the first time, the DoT became undeniably cognisant of the gulf between its enactments and the standards achieved in practice. By 1993 TRANSEC had become an effective organization.

Then it fell to the Treasury sword. The carefully constructed TRANSEC began to unravel. Its staff was reduced by one third, from 120 to 80, a massive cut. Most senior posts were downgraded. Some of the most able individuals lost their jobs or resigned. The reorganisation continued for an unbelievable two years (October 1993 to October 1995) during which staff morale was understandably destroyed. TRANSEC's establishment (78 in 1998), is a reflection of the priority accorded by HMG to aviation security. It is not failings by the staff of TRANSEC, nor even the reluctance of the industry, which since 1993 have inhibited progress. It is the want of priority. Ten years after Lockerbie, aviation security lacks a driving force. It has lost public and political attention in Great Britain.

The Transport Committee

Parliamentary Select Committees have no executive powers. They do have important influence in Parliament, and thus over ministers who are subject to interrogation in the House. The Transport Committee reviewed aviation security prior to Lockerbie, in 1986, and immediately after, in 1989.

Their 1986 Report contained 21 Recommendations. All were sensible. Nineteen addressed matters of detail, that is, standards. Only two addressed fundamentals – the need for an Inspectorate and the need to establish the Aviation Security Fund. Both of these Recommendations were rejected by the DoT, the former on the most dubious of grounds, a decision which was reversed immediately after Lockerbie by Paul Channon.[18]

Their 1989 Report contained 28 Recommendations. Again, all were sensible. On this occasion 13 were, in general terms, fundamental. One chided the DoT for its complicity in the system's greatest flaw: 'existing powers were poorly used', exactly the deficiency which, in the US case, had led to the loss of PanAm 103.[19] All of the remaining 15 Recommendations addressed issues of major importance, including the screening of hold baggage on international flights and the reconciliation of passengers with cabin baggage. Had the Transport Committee's 28 Recommendations been implemented promptly and effectively, Britain's aviation security standards would have been raised much higher and much sooner.

Aviation and Maritime Security Act 1990

The Aviation and Maritime Security Act replaced the previous system of statutory Directions issued under the Aviation Security Act 1982. Its main effect was to speed and simplify the process of issuing Directions, and to extend their scope over all organisations, (air cargo, supply, and other agencies), and persons (including passengers and staff) involved in aviation. There were two key provisions within the lengthy Act:

- Power to issue Enforcement Notices upon offending persons or organisations. An Enforcement Notice can prohibit operations until rectification of the deficiency.
- Inclusion of directors and other senior officers of a body corporate in the guilt for a corporate offence.

This latter provision was important. It placed liability where it belonged: upon directors or others who ordered, encouraged, or neglected to see breaches of security within their organisation.

The Aviation and Maritime Security Act did not seek to address the details of the aviation security. It was intended to provide the system with an effective legislative basis.

The Conduct of HMG

It was the experience of BALPA that HMG conducted all stages of the administrative and legislative process with integrity and competence.

At NASC BALPA was able to comment on current issues. By virtue of the extensive operations of its membership, it was generally much better informed as to the realities of aviation security standards, both domestic and overseas, than was the DoT or the industry. NASC members are able to submit papers to the Committee, and BALPA took full advantage of this. BALPA papers always advocated higher standards and thus translated into demands for greater activity by the DoT. The DoT, by virtue of its limited resources and the challenge already facing it, rarely welcomed additional responsibilities. Nonetheless, it always tabled a written reply, thereby opening the debate. This is significant because the best blocking tactic, much utilised by industry, is to avoid discussion of an issue, by failure, delay or obfuscation in reply. After Lockerbie, and in response to Paul Channon's request, BALPA submitted a 24-page document containing 27 recommendations. To each of these the DoT replied, recording its position and thus offering it for criticism.

The first recourse for an organisation which finds itself in disagreement with a government department is to seek the intervention of the appropriate minister. This is no easy task as ministers have great pressures on their time. Nonetheless several ministers found time to meet BALPA and listen to its concerns on aviation security. In one case, the need for a security incident reporting system, ministers (Michael Portillo and Patrick McLoughlin) accepted the advice of BALPA in preference to that of the DoT. In the matter of achieving passenger-cabin baggage reconciliation another minister was not persuaded to act, and the deficiency went unremedied. All meetings served a useful purpose in that they served to draw the ministers' attention to the subject of aviation security. Thus an organisation with a legitimate interest in a subject was, with perseverance, generally able to obtain access to the minister.

The second recourse is to lobby members of parliament. They can, if convinced of the merits of the case, put down questions which a minister is obliged to answer. The answers are drafted by his department, which in turn is obliged to rethink its position. When a Bill is passing through parliament, it is reviewed in Standing Committee. Members of the Committee are able to amend the Bill, which provides a good opportunity to seek support for suggestions of improvements. During the passage of the Aviation and Maritime Security Bill, members of the three main parties made themselves available to BALPA and subsequently supported the amendment which it advocated. At no time did any member seek to make political capital out of aviation security. In fact two Labour MPs, Gwyneth Dunwoody and Peter Snape, at the time in opposition, gave good advice on how to avoid politicisation in order to achieve the desired change. Similarly, through the good offices of Lord Clinton-Davies, at the time Vice-President of BALPA, the Association was able to inform the Lords of its concerns.

The activity of the Transport Committee is an important strand in the conduct of HMG. The Committee is all-party and has a quasi-independent role. Both of its reports on aviation security were full of good sense. The 1989 Report came close to the heart of a number of fundamental issues. The Committee hears the views of all parties which have a legitimate interest. It has the added advantage of access to the intelligence services, MI5 and MI6, which can give briefings on confidential matters. The Committee is therefore likely to be better informed on the subject than any other single body. BALPA submitted a comprehensive document and 27 recommendations to the 1989 Committee, the bulk of which were adopted.

The loss of Pan Am 103 constitutes powerful evidence for the importance of government attention to well-informed submissions. One of BALPA's key recommendations to HMG was that the final decision on matters of security, as on matters of safety, must rest with the aircraft Captain. Had the Captain of Pan Am 103 been informed that a passenger had failed to board at Heathrow, his investigation might well have revealed that prevailing security regulations had not been correctly applied. Had the Captain of Pan Am 103A been accurately appraised of the security standards at Frankfurt, he too would have investigated. Either of the two Captains, given the information and authority demanded by BALPA, would have been in a position to have averted the loss.

HMG, at all levels, showed itself open to advice and representation. BALPA was continually asked by Pilots Associations of countries as diverse as France and Hong Kong, for advice on achieving similar access to government. The failings of aviation security in Great Britain were not failings of openness of government. They were failings of strategic management skills, and of the Conservative government dogma of costs lying where they fall. They were failings of greatness.

British Aviation Security Ten years after Lockerbie

Using the same simple framework as before indicates that many and great improvements were prompted by the atrocity at Lockerbie, but that serious weaknesses still remain.

Political direction is paramount to a nation's system of aviation security. It reflects the government's sense of responsibility and its managerial competence. The effectiveness of the system rests upon the priority and resources allocated to it. It was suggested that, pre-Lockerbie, there were three conceptual flaws in the political direction: lack of a strategy, absence of a command structure, and government failure to accept responsibility to contribute to the costs.

Government sources now claim that a command structure is in place. The nature of the structure is not a matter which the government would wish to discuss publicly, therefore the claim cannot be verified. It is not likely that Britain's highly competent civil service would have failed to address the major deficiency in command which was revealed in the Sheriff's Determination. However it is not clear that there is a central point of command, nor that the new structure would be suited to higher levels of activity.

It is clear that the previous Conservative administration had been blunt in its denial of any financial responsibility for aviation security. It presided over the dismemberment of TRANSEC. It introduced an Air Passenger Duty which will contribute an estimated £700m. to government revenue (1997-98). Given that aviation security costs to British airlines are broadly estimated to be over £200m. annually, the industry can be forgiven the cynical view that it is being used as a stand-in defence budget as well as a stand-in target for the government. This is no foundation for the partnership which would best serve the interests of aviation security. Industry may well hope that the new Labour administration will bring a new sense of government responsibility. At present one of the original conceptual flaws is perpetuated by its absence.

This flaw, *per se,* is part of the evidence that a second conceptual flaw, the absence of a holistic approach, remains uncorrected. Absence of strategy translates into ill-defined objectives pursued with inappropriate resources. Before Lockerbie, this was manifest in laxity in command, in the piecemeal patching up of standards, and in failure to obtain compliance with standards. In 1998 its manifestation is different. The aviation security system is much improved. Terminals have been reconstructed, hold baggage screening has been introduced, security agents are achieving greatly improved standards. Industry has spent more than £1b, but the fact that the government made no contribution to huge capital costs is more a past than a present problem. The present problem is that the government does not wish to recognise that the industry faces competition from foreign airlines not carrying the same security overheads, either because their governments assist by one means or another, or because they are based in countries with a lax approach to security. To add safety insult to security injury, they may well be operating early iron-age Illyushin or Tupelov aircraft under European flags of convenience.

Manifestations of absence of strategy may change, although in 1992 BALPA had already drawn HMG attention to the effect of government policy on the industry's competitiveness. Whatever the manifestation, the root cause remains. Until HMG takes a holistic view of security – which includes the industry's economic perspective – neither the interests of aviation security nor the interests of Britain's civil aviation industry will be optimised.

The administrative system has undergone two major and several minor reorganisations since 1988.

• Those who advocate a higher level of activity and competence in aviation security would say that the DoT remains under-resourced both in number and in seniority of its staff establishment. It is certainly true that the DoT is currently criticised, on occasion savagely, by industry for failing to understand the realities of aviation operation and of commerce. However resources should be derived from whatever objectives emerge from the formulation of strategy. In the absence of formulation and agreement on strategy by HMG and industry, disagreement on HMG resources is a subordinate issue.

- The rank of DoT aviation security officials is governed by the civil service career structure. The fact remains that the staff should be of a calibre to earn the respect of their opposite numbers in industry.
- The DoT inspection and audit programme established by TRANSEC in the aftermath of Lockerbie has made a significant contribution to improvements in standards and to the inculcation of security consciousness.
- The DoT is still criticised by industry for its lack of expertise in aviation. Certainly TRANSEC recruits from the civil service rather than from the industry.
- The DoT has addressed the issue of non-compliance. Unfortunately, enactments drafted to ensure a suitable basis for legal action tend towards legal prose, i.e. incomprehensibility.
- BALPA reports that levels of compliance have steadily improved since the establishment of TRANSEC.

The Standards have undergone a transformation since 1988.

- One hundred per cent hold baggage screening is close to implementation at major British airports. Systems are automated, with handsearch available as a last resort. The introduction of the system was in itself a success story. It was managed by industry, not the DoT. The British Airport Authority's management skills resulted in the final cost of implementation at its seven airports, which include Heathrow and Gatwick, being £200m, against the original estimate of £400m.
- Reconciliation of passengers with their cabin baggage is now in place. However it was not until 1995 that this was achieved, despite the best efforts of BALPA. Some airlines were unco-operative, at least one deliberately so, and the DoT did not have the aviation or management expertise to overcome their obstruction.
- Security of cargo and supplies has been addressed. In essence, the method is to establish the probity of the agent and to charge him with guaranteeing the security of his material.
- Serious gaps in the integrity of the total security system have been closed.

Security consciousness and commitment has developed. Security is now widely accepted as a part of aviation's routine. BALPA reports that pilots seeking to implement security procedures do not now (1998) face the opposition from management that once was common in certain airlines. However, it cannot be said that that security is as deeply and permanently embedded in aviation's consciousness as is safety. During the twenty years prior to Lockerbie, attacks on European and US aviation occurred with regularity, often accompanied by atrocities. They provided regular reminders of the importance of security. One of the products of successful security and the diminution of attacks is that the need for security may become less obvious to HMG and aviation managers, and that their unconcern may transmit itself to aviation staff. Commitment to aviation security can only follow the example set by those who direct it.

The security of British aircraft overseas founders on the iceberg of host-state responsibility. In the matter of their national sovereignty, nations display a degree of *amour propre* which, in a person, would invite committal to an asylum. International enactments, whether of ICAO, ECAC or other, rely on individual host-states for translation into the reality of security practice. Any failure of implementation can only be addressed by diplomatic representations. After Lockerbie, many British embassies appointed an official to monitor and encourage host-states' aviation security standards. The officials were well-placed to perform a valuable service. Unfortunately, such is the difficulty of achieving the rectification of deficiencies in other nations' standards, there are signs of HMG ceasing to make the effort. When the DOT's Principal Inspector (Overseas) retired in 1993, his post was downgraded. DoT's programme of overseas inspection has now diminished to zero. Similar pressures and those of the budget threaten the important work undertaken by Foreign Office officials abroad. Thus the issue of the security of British aircraft overseas, which is so intractable that HMG wishes to disengage itself, is left to British airlines to pursue locally as best they can.

The way forward is for like-minded countries to establish building blocks for progress, in the form of bilateral and similar alliances. Each would have to operate an aviation security regime in which the other/s could be confident. The alliances would then work in harmony at international level to persuade other nations to display similar responsibility.

Twenty years after Lockerbie, HMG along with most other governments, is allocating little priority to the pursuit of progress in overseas security standards. The charitable will point to the inherent difficulties of the subject. The less charitable will point out that the difficulties are the very reason for which it should be allocated more resources, not less.

Conclusion

By many measures Great Britain's civil aviation industry is the third largest in the world, after the USA and the CIS. Most other countries therefore face an easier task in pursuing high standards of aviation security. Few, possibly none, have performed as well as Great Britain. Many have neither active terrorist enemies nor do they have Great Britain's profile in world affairs. They, therefore, do not perceive themselves to be facing a serious threat. As a result, they have little commitment to aviation security. Others who face a higher threat have not demonstrated the combination of commitment and competence which translates into the achievement of higher standards.

In the five years following Lockerbie, there is no doubt that Great Britain showed both commitment and competence. However, HMG has not at any time adopted a truly holistic approach to the threat of terrorist and other attacks on aviation. HMG has not acknowledged its own central responsibility for bringing the threat of attack upon its industry. For as long as HMG holds firmly to the convenient fiction that it has no financial responsibility for security countermeasures, industry will resist the argument that its duty to care for its passengers constitutes a blank cheque for the government.

Since Lockerbie, HMG has chosen to proceed by a system of edict and enforcement. It has produced a regime much inferior to that which would have resulted from a partnership. HMG and industry have different resources and abilities. HMG has intellect, intelligence services, diplomatic expertise and command of government resources. The industry has a knowledge of aviation and management expertise unmatched by government. The different strengths of HMG and industry are a text-book case of potential synergy. There is no evidence of HMG seeking to harness those strengths into a partnership. Great Britain as a whole is the loser.

In 1988 the atrocity of Lockerbie drew media, public and

government attention to aviation security. It prompted HMG to conduct a review which, albeit not strategic, produced excellent results. Ten years after Lockerbie, attention has wandered from aviation security. For a government to engage a difficult subject in response to public demand is democracy. To be driven to the same subject by a sense of responsibility is statesmanship.

A strategic review of aviation security must address the good of Great Britain as a whole. It is a project in which HMG and industry must be partners if existing conceptual flaws are to be corrected. Such a review has never been undertaken in Great Britain. It would be demanded by the country if there were another Lockerbie. Better to conduct it now, and perhaps prevent the next atrocity. There could be no better memorial to the victims of Pan Am 103.

NOTES

1. Since 1988 the Department has re-engineered its name at intervals, from DTp to DoT to DTp to DETR. The term DoT is used throughout this paper.
2. Claire Sterling, *The Terror Network* (London: Weidenfeld & Nicholson, 1981), p.114
3. David Phillips, *Skyjack* (London: Harrap, 1973), pp.130–1.
4. Leila Khaled, *My People Shall Live* (London: Hodder & Stoughton, 1973), p.126
5. Phillips (note 3), pp.130–1.
6. John Laffin, *Fedayeen* (London: Cassell, 1973), pp.48–9.
7. David Leppard, *On The Trail of Terror* (London: Cape, 1991), recommended for an account of the investigation
8. Determination by the Sheriff Principal John S Mowat QC in the Fatal Accident Inquiry relating to the Lockerbie Air Disaster, 1991.
9. Report of the President's Commission on Aviation Security and Terrorism, 1990, p.3
10. Reconciliation is the industry term for ensuring that a passenger's bag is accompanied on to the aircraft by its owner. The assumption is that the owner will not wish to destroy an aircraft in which he is travelling.
11. Determination. p.90 (note 8).
12. Ibid., pp.91–2.
13. Ibid., p.92.
14. Paul Wilkinson, *The Lessons of Lockerbie* (London : RISCT, 1989) is recommended for its careful contemporary study of the same issue.
15. Ibid., p.73.
16. Submission to the Select Committee, BALPA, March 1989, para 25 and 26
17. By convention, the *target* is the object of a terrorist's hostility, the *victim* is the unfortunate who is attacked to express that hostility. Thus at Lockerbie, the USA was the target and Pan Am 103 the victim.
18. Transport Committee. Government Response to the Fourth Report of the Committee, Session 1985–86 Edinburgh: HMSO, 1986, paras 25–28.
19. Transport Committee. Third Report, Aviation Security. HC 509, 1989, para 3.

10

A Statement on Behalf of the UK Families Group – Flight 103

JIM SWIRE

> On a huge hill, cragged and steep,
> TRUTH stands and he that will reach her about must,
> and about must go.
> *John Donne (1571–1631)*

In June 1985, 329 people died, when an Air India Boeing 747 of was lost 90 miles off Cork, Ireland. Flying from Canada, it carried a hold-bag containing an Improvised Explosive Device (IED), with automatic trigger, transferred from a connecting flight. The passenger responsible for the bag was not aboard. There was no 'Mayday' call: Raymond Davis, then head of the Flight Recorder section of the British AAIB, commented that there was no evidence that an explosion had caused the crash.[1] Meanwhile, in Tokyo's Narita airport at almost the same time, a suitcase intended for another Air India plane exploded, killing two baggage handlers, and revealing much about the likely size of the bomb which had exploded off Cork.

On 21 December 1988, the Pan Am 747 *Maid of the Seas* had flown in from the USA. Loaded from empty at Heathrow, she received baggage and passengers from 'interline' and feeder-flight sources, as

Dr Swire would like to thank the members of 'UK Families-Flight 103' who supported the writing of this article. Also all those who have listened objectively to us over the years and our many friends and supporters, academic, professional, political, lay, and in the media, in the UK and abroad, alive or no longer with us, who have helped, informed and kept hope alive. Their support has helped to ensure that those who died are remembered with honour and respect, and that their passing may not have been utterly in vain.

Meanwhile we still 'about must, and about must go', for there is still so much to be done.

well as those initiating their journey at Heathrow.[2] Now designated 'Pan Am Flight 103', her feeder-flight, a Boeing 727 from Frankfurt was designated 'Pan Am Flight 103A'. A 727, unlike a 747, does not carry the hold-bags in containers, so the Frankfurt bags were loaded loose into the 747 containers in the terminal, then left unguarded awaiting further luggage. Next door to the Pan Am facility in 1988 was the facility used by Iran-Air. Nobody knew whether the bags from the Frankfurt flight had their passengers with them.[3] Despite the dire warning of Air India, the passage of three years and the recommendations of the UN's International Civil Aviation Organisation (ICAO,)[4] the United Kingdom was not to lead the world in hold baggage security until 1997, when full 'baggage reconciliation' – the matching of each hold-bag with a verified on-board passenger, or with a special security procedure – was finally made fully mandatory for all international flights from or through the UK.[5]

Even then, Joanna Walters in *The Observer* ('Chaos Prompts Airport Pledge', 31 August 1997) wrote:

> Airports owner BAA is to invest up to £250 million to improve its baggage systems at Heathrow ... after thousands of bags were lost during the August travel peak.

This was eight-and-a-half years after BAA (Heathrow) had loaded an unaccompanied case with the subsequent death of 270 innocent people.

In the week before Christmas it is notoriously difficult to get seats to popular destinations, yet only about two-thirds of the 747's seats were filled.[6] A number of passengers, including the writer's 23 year-old daughter, had booked at the last moment, surprised at their 'luck' in getting a seat. At 7.03 pm, in the winter dark over Lockerbie at a height of 31,000 ft, a small IED in a Toshiba cassette recorder, containing some 350 grams of 'Semtex' high velocity explosive, detonated in the forward cargo-hold just in front of the port wing-root, among bags originating from Frankfurt.[7]

Instantly, a petalled hole was blown in the fuselage skin, but the shock wave associated with the high ignition velocity of the Semtex, travelled round inside the fuselage circumference and, helped by the stress imposed by the pressurisation, severed the forward fuselage from the rest of the aircraft. The beheaded corpse of the aircraft went into a steepening dive, with consequent secondary disintegration. The central wing assembly, carrying about thirty tons of fuel, excavated a huge crater in the town of Lockerbie below.[8] and created a fireball which vapourised several houses with their occupants and ignited others. There were no survivors aboard and eleven Lockerbie residents were killed on the ground. Disruption had again been so abrupt that even the cockpit sound-recorder carried only a split second of abnormal noise.[9] Thus ended the lives of 270 people from 21 separate nations, with an average age of only 27.

A dedicated search of the crash site, extending right across the Borders to the North Sea, was organised under the Dumfries and Galloway police force, complicated by the immediate arrival of some unidentified Americans, who appeared to interfere with potentially 'evidential' material, and even perhaps bodies, in the first few days. From the start the police had designated this as a murder inquiry.[10]

As in any murder investigation there must be a motive. Libya had been bombed by the Americans in 1986, in response to the 'LaBelle' disco bombing in Germany, in which two Americans died. Six months before Lockerbie, an Iranian airbus had been destroyed by the American 'Aegis' class missile cruiser 'Vincennes'. Iran openly vowed that 'the skies would rain blood on America' in revenge. America's hostages were held by Iranian groups, and in the words of one world expert on Aviation Security '… It is generally accepted that revenge for the destruction of the Iranian airbus was the basis for the attack in 1988 on the Pan American jumbo jet over Lockerbie.'[11]

Meanwhile America was still licking the wounds left by the 'Iran-Contra' scandal, and George Bush, running for president, realised the political potential of recovering the hostages, the last of whom were not released until after the blame for Lockerbie was publicly placed on Libya, in 1991.

Among the wreckage were found fragments of circuit board, pieces of a suitcase, and shreds of clothing which, investigators claimed, established that the bomb had been built into a Toshiba tape recorder placed among clothing originating from Malta, and contained in a 'Samsonite' hard suitcase.

The world's aviation experts had had three years to exploit the findings of the Air India disaster, which they tried hard to do through ICAO, whose recommendations were ignored and mandatory demands only very slowly attended to by 'contracting states'. A spectacular series of warnings – ten are known to us at present – had been received in the West.[12]

One warning was supplied to all interested parties in November 1988 through Interpol. It was a pamphlet giving details of an 'IED' specifically designed for use against aircraft in flight, being triggered by a barometric transducer.[13] it also warned that there might be more similar bombs as yet unaccounted for. In addition it pointed out that the X-Ray technology of the day would be virtually unable to differentiate between a normal recorder and the IED.

The bomb had been recovered from the boot of a car in which the leaders of a terrorist cell, part of the Syrian-based group known as the Popular Front for the Liberation of Palestine – General Command (PFLP-GC), had been arrested, near Frankfurt airport. Their overall leader was the Syrian, Ahmed Jibril, a close associate of President Assad of Syria. Inexplicably the Germans had released 14 of the 16 cell members, within days, and the two remaining in custody were never charged with plotting to blow up an aircraft in flight. It was not until 1989 that the Germans discovered a further cache of IEDs made by this group. They seem to have had multiple targets.

The Head of British Aviation Security, James Jack, received this warning and sent out his assessment.[15] Incredibly he commented that:

> Any item about which a searcher is unable to satisfy himself/herself must, if it is to be carried in the aircraft, be consigned to the aircraft hold.

Perhaps the British were so absorbed by the spate of air-hijackings which had marked the previous decade, and where devices/weapons must be in the passenger cabin, that they were unable to adjust to the thought of in-flight sabotage bombings. But the words of Professor Paul Wilkinson written a year after Lockerbie, in the light of early changes made to UK security (despite the governmental denial of any fault), are more hard hitting

> Even with its new Aviation Security Inspectorate, the Department of Transport is ... in far too cosy a relationship with vested commercial interests in the transport business ... for whom all other considerations including security must be subordinated to the profit motive.[16]

In those days a major UK airline was even a significant contributor to the funds of the Conservative party.

The subsequent Fatal Accident Inquiry (Scottish inquest) was forbidden to look at the intelligence scene, or fully to assess Government provision for aviation security.[17] It was also required to avoid evidence relevant to the still ongoing criminal investigation. Both the Prime Minister (Margaret Thatcher) and the Transport Secretary (Paul Channon) refused to attend the FAI as witnesses. The author, after a decision to represent himself at the FAI, was specifically prevented from returning to an examination of security at Heathrow.[18] The FAI did, however, conclude that the Lockerbie aircraft was under 'The Host State Protection' of the UK.

Later, in her book *The Downing Street Years*, Mrs Thatcher was to write of her support for the bombing of Tripoli and Bengazi, that 'The much vaunted Libyan counter attack did not and could not occur'.[19] When asked by the author why, in that case, her government had assured the relatives that Libya was responsible for Lockerbie, she wrote, 'I have nothing to add to the text'. She also denied a press report that she had agreed with president Bush 'to play Lockerbie low-key'.[20]

There has been no objective inquiry into why UK security and intelligence performed in the way that they did in 1988. The relatives persuaded a subsequent Transport Secretary (Lord Parkinson) that an inquiry into the failures should be set up. His request was rejected by Mrs Thatcher (and her cabinet). Thus the figure ultimately responsible for the protection of her citizens refused to authorise any comprehensive inquiry, despite the desperately serious allegations being voiced by the relatives. This degree of immunity cannot be healthy for the future performance of intelligence and aviation security, and is an added torture for the families. 'Quis custodiet ipsos custodienses?'

However, despite a background of denying fault, but under continuing pressure, from the UK relatives, there have been enormous changes in UK Aviation security since Lockerbie. They have been inordinately slow, and no heads have rolled for the mess in 1988. They have significantly reduced the likelihood of a further 'Lockerbie' happening to an aircraft on an international flight, originating from or stopping off in, the UK. The same cannot be said of Aviation Security in other countries, notably the USA. Nor is there is any such reassurance concerning UK intelligence. One of the more telling comments from the Sheriff Principal in charge of the Fatal Accident Inquiry was:

Mr Jack (the Head of Aviation Security) was entitled to rely on the absence of an urgent assessment from the security services as an indication that the threat was not serious.[21]

No urgent assessment ever came: why not?

During the intervening ten years, the relatives have obtained the text of ten warnings, not one of them volunteered by the authorities.[22] At the time of writing, we are continuing to press the 'New Labour' government to appoint a suitable board of inquiry.[23] It will have to be led by a figure of unimpeachable impartiality, for some of its work would have to be conducted *in camera.* The new government has no responsibility for what happened in 1988, but has an obligation to protect its citizens in future and to promote justice.

Meanwhile the criminal investigation was continuing. It was claimed that the bomb had been loaded aboard an Air Malta flight from Luqa to Frankfurt by two 'Libyan intelligence agents'.[24] At Frankfurt it is said to have been transferred from Air Malta to the Pan Am feeder flight '103A' for Heathrow, where, the story goes, it was duly loaded into one of the 747's baggage containers.

This story has been seriously challenged since being used to justify indictments against two Libyans on 14 November 1991. The Head of the FBI explosives laboratory, James T. Thurman, who claimed, on camera,[25] to have made the link between a fragment of circuit board from the wreckage and a piece of timer circuit board used 'only by the Libyans' has been transferred from his post following allegations of improper use of evidence in other FBI murder cases.[26] The circuit board compared by him with the fragment appears to have been provided to him by the CIA. Inevitably 'conspiracy theories', fuelled by the unusually low load-factor for Flight 103 and the German find of further IEDs in 1989, have sprung up, as to whether one act of revenge, instead of the six she seemed to be seeking was 'allowed' to Iran in exchange for political favours.

Investigative journalists soon discovered that the firm that had manufactured the circuit board had also supplied timers to the East German Stazi.[27] The Stazi had acted as trainers for a number of terrorist groups including the PFLP-GC. The timings of alleged actions by the two Libyan suspects in Malta appear to be inaccurate. A major research effort for a film 'The Maltese Double Cross', funded by the late Tiny Rowland, whose international business interests included Libya and most other African countries, produced credible alternative explanations, notably for the presence of 'Malta derived clothing' among the bomb debris. Both the film and its contributors were viciously attacked here and in the US.[28]

When Granada television screened a programme based on the 'official version', they were sued by Air Malta who denied that the bomb could have been carried on their aircraft. Granada settled out of Court.[29] Furthermore, the UK relatives had been told by Scotland's then Lord Advocate, Lord Fraser, that Germany had been providing 'unprecedented support' to the criminal investigation. Yet their correspondence with the Germans produced a letter from Chancellor Kohl's office, dated 6 March 1996, stating, (in a certified commercial translation) that:

> The Federal Government is aware that there is still the suspicion expressed in various quarters that the explosive which caused the Pan Am aircraft to crash was carried from Frankfurt to London. However – as the Federal Ministry of Justice has emphatically assured me – there is nothing to indicate this. The investigations carried out by the Frankfurt Public Prosecutor's Office in connection with the crash, which also concentrated on this question specifically, produced no findings to support this view.[30]

As the well known British QC, Michael Mansfield, commented, referring to the available evidence as to what happened in Malta:

> Were it to be presented to a court in the United Kingdom it probably wouldn't even get past the door, it would be declared at some stage or other 'inadmissible evidence', because it is so fatally flawed … Fundamentally you have to be able to show an evidential link between those accused and the incident itself. There has to be continuity of evidence and there has to be a link of causation. One examines closely what was found at Lockerbie, at the scene of the crime … then you work back to Heathrow, … what could take us back unequivocally from Heathrow to Frankfurt? … then at Frankfurt the same exercise has to be undergone to take us unequivocally back to Malta … it's all based on this one premise that it was put on in Malta … it seems on a CIA approach to life you can't win unless you've got a particular hypothesis which is theirs – namely 'the Libyans did it, therefore everything else flows from it'.[31]

A simpler solution was proposed by one of the co-founders of Iranian overseas intelligence, Abolhassem Mesbahi, who defected to Germany in 1997.[32] He confirmed that Lockerbie was a revenge attack by Iran, named certain individuals who were involved, and claimed that the bomb had been brought to Heathrow by an Iran-Air flight, primed there, and inserted in the baggage container. The evidence must be subjected to the test of a fair criminal court. Until then we do not know whether the whole Libyan story is a red-herring. Certain it is that those who originated the plot remain free.

Following the issue of the indictments, the Security Council passed resolutions 'demanding the surrender' of the accused to Scotland or America for trial and imposing sanctions on Libya.[33] The Montreal Convention of 1971, signed by all three nations, provides specifically for such a situation of aviation terrorism.[34] Under its article 7, it is clear that Libya has the right to try the two accused herself. Libya turned to the World Court to decide whether the Security Council had exceeded its powers in demanding that the trial take place only in the UK or US.[35] The court decided that it did have jurisdiction to decide this issue. Its verdict may be made known in the first half of 1999.

Meanwhile a Professor of Scots law, Robert Black of Edinburgh University, drew up a proposal for trial under the normal rules and practices of Scottish criminal law, but with an International panel of judges, led by a Scottish judge appointed by the British Prime Minister, to replace the jury, and to sit in a neutral country.[36] This proposal was accepted by the Libyans in 1994.[37] It was also accepted by the UK relatives as providing a fair locus for the trial, in lieu of their first choice, trial in Scotland, which time had shown the sanctions impotent to achieve.[38] The relatives also noted that Professor Black's proposed court met the criticism raised in late 1997 by President Nelson Mandela of South Africa that 'No one nation should be complainant, prosecutor and judge', since the panel of judges would be international, rather than Scottish. His proposal was for five judges, and specified that the 'lead judge' must be Scottish, in order that he could instruct the others in the functioning of Scottish Criminal law. A representative of the UK relatives, together with Professor Black, revisited Libya gaining the approval of the Libyan leader, government and lawyers for this solution in April 1998.[39] The Libyans reaffirmed their acceptance of the Professor's proposed court and appeared willing to allow the Secretary General of the United Nations to appoint the other four judges. Within hours the US State Department had commented:

> We have no doubt that this latest Libyan agreement reflects a
> desire to evade its obligations rather than a willingness to see
> justice done.[40]

In fact the Libyans doubted the fairness of a jury trial, the Professor's
proposed court has no jury, and in 1997 it received enormous
encouragement from UN Inspectors invited to Scotland to look at the
fairness of the Scottish criminal system. In their report they
commented:

> The system of criminal justice in Scotland depends essentially
> upon the proposition that jurors … should arrive in the jury box
> without knowledge of facts or alleged facts relating to the crime
> charged … If the accused could reasonably establish that their
> right to a free(fair?) trial would be prejudiced by a jury trial, we
> suggest that the idea of dispensing with the jury be pursued with
> the Government of the United Kingdom.[41]

Modern media penetration, as in a developed country like Scotland,
may have rendered jury trial unsafe for any such high profile cases in
future.

'UK Families-Flight 103' came together to form a group to support
its members in their grief, and has produced friendships which will last
a lifetime. The way our members were treated by 'the authorities'
helped to unite us, but deepened our need and distress. Some of us have
become dedicated to finding the truth. Some have tried quietly to return
to a 'normal' life again. Some of us come regularly to meetings, others
rely on the excellent summaries from our co-ordinator. All of us are
seeking to cope with our grief in our individual ways. Sadly we have
seen a number of our members, of whom we had grown so fond,
succumb to stress-related diseases.

Many of our families found that they were interrogated again and
again. The investigators needed to know about the dead, their friends
and possible links to suspect organisations. But to have to face this
intrusive questioning five times or more, caused intense distress to
some, and undermined our confidence in those conducting the inquiry.

A trained person allocated to each family, and trusted by both us and
the authorities could have been a great help. We were law-abiding
citizens and out of our depth. Sheer frustration has since made us bold.

At the (obligatory) FAI, some of us found that our wishes were being ignored by those who represented us. They were following a course designed to maximise financial compensation, but refusing, without explanation, to call other witnesses who we wanted cross-examined. Many felt that they were treated as a nuisance on the periphery of an 'incident', which 'belonged' not to us but to the 'professionals'. No one conferred with us as to the relative importance we attached to finding the truth, as opposed to maximising the compensation. Only later did we find out enough about the lawyer-client relationship to realise that there was no need to tolerate such rebuffs, nor to allow the lawyers to keep 30 per cent of the final awards. In the later TWA disaster 10 per cent was agreed.

There was persistent refusal to allow any relatives to see the bodies, coupled with a slowly unrolling saga of bodies left lying in the open at the crash site for days. Confusion over the dates on death certificates – some said the 24 December instead of the 21 December – when eventually issued, was a new horror: (had any victims lain in the open mortally injured but unnoticed, some wondered) it was also entirely avoidable.

We are proud that some of our members have made notable contributions at conferences, in print, and in the other media outlets,[42] towards improving knowledge of the needs of families caught up in such disasters in future, and that our right to truth and justice has been so widely proclaimed. We remain determined to force some gain out of so great a loss. The memory of those who died must be honoured.

At the individual level our members can recall so many acts of kindness and consideration from friends, individual police officers and lawyers, social workers, local people in Lockerbie, even total strangers around the world. But the further up one looks in the UK hierarchy the more does one become disillusioned. There has been no admission that things could have been done better, nor has there been any apology.

Even the Lockerbie Air Disaster Fund was wound up against our protests that it should be kept open to fund support for long term effects of stress among emergency service, police and military personnel, as well as relatives. A suggestion borne out by several sad stories since.

The FAI held that the plane was under the Host State protection of the UK authorities.[43] At the time of writing (August 1998), no Prime Minister has yet met with our group despite repeated requests. On 21 December 1992 we gathered in Downing Street for a prearranged meeting with

Prime Minister, John Major, only to watch, shivering on the pavement nearly half an hour later, as he drove past us in his official car.

Tragically, the handling of the Lockerbie case seems even to have endangered the reputation of the UN and Security Council under Article 7. This has driven 'UK Families-Flight 103', in their search for justice, to seek the help of regional organisations such as the Arab League and OAU, and of other countries with influence, such as China and Russia.
If the UN's own World Court decides in favour of the Montreal Convention and against such use of the Security Council by veto-wielding members in future, that would strengthen respect for both the UN and international treaties. If not, perhaps those treaties should all carry codicils to the effect that they need only be honoured if the Security Council of the day says so. That seems to put politics above the law.

At the time of writing it does appear that the US and UK are now prepared to consider trial in a neutral country, and that the Dutch Government may have agreed to such a trial being held at The Hague. This remarkable and most welcome development may have been triggered by the increasingly evident isolation in which the UK and US found themselves. The Organisation of African Unity issued an ultimatum in June 1998, that 'if the US/UK refuse that the two suspects be tried in a third, neutral country ... the OAU will no longer comply with security Council Resolutions 748 and 883 ... with effect from September1998.'[44] Meanwhile in March 1998 all but three of the fifty or so nations represented in an open meeting of the UN Security Council had criticised the Anglo-US position.

Unfortunately, the discussions held by the UN in Rome, in June 1998, to define a Permanent International Criminal Court, were so weakened by various objections that no specific provision for dealing with international terrorism was achieved.

The best hope of getting justice over Lockerbie therefore currently remains a court to try the accused under Scottish Criminal law, most probably sitting in The Hague, having a panel of judges instead of a jury, but otherwise imbued with all the powers of sentence and appeal normally available to such a court sitting in Scotland. That, and objective inquiry into the apparent Intelligence failures of 1988 remain prime objectives for the members of 'UK Families-Flight 103'.

NOTES

1. *Toronto Globe and Mail* newspaper – quoted by Rodney Wallis, *Combating Air Terrorism* (London: Brasseys, 1993), p.6.
2. Determination of Lockerbie Fatal Accident Inquiry, Dumfries, Scotland (Published 18 March 1991, Airdrie Sheriff Principal's Chambers).
3. Ibid.
4. ICAO – Security – International standards and Recommended Practices Annex 17 Fourth Ed., October 1989: 4.3.1 and Note following.
5. UK Department of Transport order, 'fully mandatory' from March 1997.
6. Report of President's Commission on Aviation Security and Terrorism (Washington DC USA Executive Order 12686, 4 August 1989.)
7. UK Air Accident Investigation report into the Lockerbie disaster. Air Accident Investigation 2/90, London, HMSO – ISBN 0-11-550981-X – 11 Sept.1990.
8. Ibid.
9. Ibid.
10. See note 2.
11. Wallis (see note 1).
12. Documents in possession of 'UK Families-Flight 103'
13. Ibid.
14. Ibid.
15. Ibid.
16. Paul Wilkinson, 'The Lessons of Lockerbie', Conflict Studies 226 (London: Research Institute on the Study of Conflict and Terrorism, December 1989).
17. See note 2.
18. Ibid.
19. Margaret Thatcher, *The Downing Street Years* (London: HarperCollins, 1993), p.449.
20. See note 12.
21. See note 2.
22. See note 12.
23. August 1998.
24. 'Fact Sheet' by US State Department. 'Additional Information on the Bombing of Pan Am Flight 103', 15 November 1991, and Indictments issued by United States District Court of Columbia (Grand Jury), 14 November 1991.
25. Video in possession of 'UK Families-Flight 103' from ABC News.
26. Allegations by Dr Frederick Whitehurst (FBI) and report of the American Department of Justice Investigation. See 'Tainting Evidence', Kelly and Wearne (USA: Simon & Schuster, 1998).
27. MEBO Ltd, Badenerstrasse 414, 8004 Zurich, Switzerland. Director: Edwin Bollier.
28. Film *The Maltese Double Cross*, Copyright: available from Hemar Enterprises, 21 Brondersbury Villas, London, NW6 6AH.
29. Grenada settlement: Norton Rose, Solicitors for Air Malta, November 1993.
30. See note 12.
31. *Frontline Scotland*, BBC Scotland, Broadcasting House, Queen Margaret Drive, Glasgow, G12 8DG, Scotland.
32. See note 12.
33. United Nations, New York, Security Council Resolutions 748 (1992) and 883 (1993)
34. Montreal Convention; Convention for the Suppression of Unlawful Acts Against the Safety of Civil Aviation, Montreal, Canada, 23 September 1971.
35. International Court of Justice(ICJ) of the UN, Den Hague Holland, also called 'The World Court'.
36. Professor Robert Black, Professor of Scots Law, University of Edinburgh, Old College, North Bridge, Edinburgh, EH8 9YL Scotland.
37. Proposal for Neutral Country Court and Libyan letter of acceptance, in possession of Professor Black (see note 36), and 'UK Families-Flight 103'.

38. However, it should be made clear that at time of going to press the US relatives were not in favour of a trial in a neutral country (*Eds*).
39. Statement issued from Tripoli, 20 April 1998, possession as note 37 above.
40 Report by *Reuters* News Service, 21 April 1998, by-line, Grant McCool
41. Report of UN Inspectors of the Scottish Judicial System, submitted to the Secretary General, Kofi Annan by Enoch Dumbutshena and Professor Henry Schermers. Forwarded to the President of the Security Council,18 December 1997.
42 See note 12.
43. See note 2.
44. Decision of the Assembly of the Heads of State of the OAU, 34th Ordinary Session, Ouagadougou, Bukina-Faso, 8-10 June 1998.

11

Enhancing Global Aviation Security?

PAUL WILKINSON

Terrorism remains the most ubiquitous form of political violence in the modern world. More than half the world's countries are directly affected every year, either by domestic or international terrorist violence, or both. There has been a welcome reduction in the annual total of incidents of international terrorism; i.e. those involving the citizens of more than one country, since the early 1990s. The bad news is that the numbers of fatalities and injuries caused by terrorist attacks have risen dramatically, and levels of domestic terrorism have risen sharply in the worst-affected countries, such as Colombia, Algeria and Sri Lanka.

There are a number of key features of the post-Cold War strategic environment that are conducive to terrorism, and hence we are likely to see high levels of this particular form of violence well into the next century. The main factors are:

1. Although the ending of the Cold War caused a major decline in ideological conflicts, bitter and protracted ethnic conflicts, many of which long predate the Cold War period, remain the most widespread underlying motivation for political violence, especially in Asia and Africa, and these conflicts frequently spawn terrorist campaigns.

2. Since the early 1980s, well before the end of the Cold War, there has been a dramatic upsurge of extreme Islamist fundamentalist movements, not only in the Middle East but throughout the Islamic world. These movements are ready to deploy the weapon of

terrorism in a self-proclaimed holy war against the United States, Israel and other western countries and with the aim of establishing 'Islamic republics' in their respective countries, based on their own fundamentalist interpretation of the Koran and the Sharia (Islamic Law).

These groups, such as Hezbollah, Hamas, the Islamic Group (Egypt), and the Armed Islamic Group (Algeria), have their own political agendas, aimed at overthrowing their particular regimes, which they see as irredeemably corrupted by the West and betraying 'true Islam', and establishing their own theocratic regimes in their place. However, all of these fundamentalist Islamist movements, whether Sunni or Shiite, have to some extent been inspired and encouraged by the success of Ayatollah Khomeini's fundamentalist Islamist revolution in Iran, and by the success of the Mujahidin in forcing the Soviets to withdraw from Afghanistan. It is a sad irony that groups of this kind, which received massive US assistance to fight the Soviet occupation of Afghanistan as part of the Reagan Doctrine during the Cold War, now constitute the most deadly international threat against the US.

3. The collapse of the former Soviet Union left the US as the sole remaining superpower. Part of the price of this lonely position is that the US is now the favourite target for all the violent groups that bitterly resent and oppose American values, culture, foreign policy and actions anywhere in the world. No less than a third of all international terrorist attacks each year are directed against US targets. The most lethal and strident of all these terrorists who perceive the US as their prime enemy are the extreme Islamist groups referred to above. These view the US as 'the Great Satan'. They blame the US for its support of Israel, the very existence of which they see as an affront to Islam, and for its past and present support of pro-Western governments in Moslem countries, which they also perceive as deadly enemies. They also bitterly oppose the Middle East peace process, and believe that the Oslo Accords between Israel and the Palestinians, which the US strongly supports, are a betrayal not only of the Palestinians but of Islamic world as a whole.

4. Thus the very existence of the Oslo Accords, designed by those who negotiated them as a route to achieving peace and stability, the bitter

hostility to them on the part of the Islamist rejectionist groups, and the failure of the US thus far to compel Prime Minister Netanyahu and his colleagues to carry out their responsibilities in implementing their side of the Oslo Accords, all serve to create conditions for continuing international terrorism linked to Middle Eastern conflicts, traditionally the most significant catalyst for the 'spillover' of international terrorism into Europe and other regions of the world.

5. Although the ending of the Cold War and the collapse of the Former Soviet Union and the East European communist regimes suddenly removed some of the key state sponsors of terrorism, this did not mean the end of state support and safe haven for terrorist groups. Iran, Iraq, Syria, Libya, and the Sudan and Afghanistan (now virtually under Taliban control) have all provided this invaluable service for a variety of terrorist groups. In the past few years, it is Iran that has been the most active state sponsor in using its terrorist clients as a tool of domestic or foreign policy.

6. A factor in facilitating the spread of terrorist activity continues to be the ready availability of weapons and explosives of all types. Moreover, in addition to the traditional sources from the international arms market and from state sponsors, the post-Cold War era has seen a major proliferation of weapons and expertise from the former Soviet Union, encouraged by a desperate need for cash and the demoralised state of the Russian military. There is serious concern that some expertise and perhaps some materials for the acquisition of weapons of mass destruction have found their way into the hands of terrorist groups or states desperate to acquire them.

7. The trends towards greater globalisation, for example in communications, electronic transfer of funds, the growth of air travel etc., have greatly facilitated the ability of terrorist groups to operate transnationally: for example, by using the Internet to disseminate their propaganda and maintain contact with supporters and sympathisers, and by creating worldwide infrastructures of financial support, arms procurement, intelligence gathering etc., to promote their terrorist campaigns. This trend is not confined to the category of transnational 'new' terrorist groups: the Tamil Tigers

and the PKK are examples of two 'old' movements that have pursued ethnic separation for more than a quarter of a century, and which have built up complex and sophisticated transnational funding and logistic support structures. Almost all protracted domestic terrorist campaigns develop an international dimension.

8. Finally, and more important than all the above factors put together, terrorism is now widely perceived as a low-cost, low-risk and high-yields method of struggle, which has a proven track record of winning valuable tactical objectives for the terrorists, such as forcing the authorities into releasing terrorists from goal, extorting large ransom demands, or publicising a cause. In sum, terrorism is viewed by those who adopt it as the natural political weapon of the weak. It is true that there are very few historical examples of terrorism succeeding in winning strategic gaols such as the overthrow of governments. The only clear cases in modern history of terrorists succeeding in their long-term political objectives are confined to the era of decolonisation struggles, from the mid-1940s to the late 1950s, when the use of terrorism as the insurgent's prime weapon against colonial rule succeeded in forcing British withdrawal from Palestine, the Canal Zone, Cyprus and Aden, and in compelling the French to negotiate Algeria's independence under the Evian Agreements. There have been no comparable victories for terrorism in the post-colonial era. Indeed, a powerful case can be made that terrorism has been an ultimately counter-productive weapon in many recent ethnic conflicts. It can certainly be demonstrated that Irish Republicans and Palestinian nationalists have secured far more by political negotiation than by terrorist campaigns that have only tended to intensify the retaliatory violence launched against them and to alienate mainstream international opinion and support. Yet, despite much evidence indicating that terrorism is a faulty weapon which often misfires, it would be foolish to underestimate its potential political impact when used under favourable conditions, such as against a weakened and divided opponent. A clear case of this in the mid-1990s was the success of militant Chechens in using mass hostage taking as a weapon to force the Russian government to concede virtual autonomy to the Chechen republic and to withdraw its forces. Moreover, whatever doubts contemporary terrorist leaders may have

about the strategic value of their campaigns of violence, the tried and tested effectiveness of terrorism in obtaining valuable short-term objectives is the decisive factor ensuring its continuing popularity as the weapon of the weak.

The 'New' International Terrorism

The combined effects of the factors in the strategic environment identified in the preceding paragraphs would alone be sufficent to ensure that the problem of terrorism continues to haunt the world well into the next century. However, there are a number of additional trends in international terrorism clearly evident in the 1990s which suggest that some of the groups involved are mutating into a potentially far more dangerous threat to international security than the groups which dominated the international terrorist scene of the 1970s and 1980s ever posed.

This 'new' international terrorism, it is argued, is more difficult to monitor and combat because it is much more amorphous and diffuse than other varieties of terrorist phenomena.[1] Instead of well-defined organizational structures, with hierarchies and chains of command common to the more traditional terrorist movements, the 'new' groups are typically part of a shadowy network of militants operating transnationally. Instead of relying on a *cadre* of professional full-time terrorists to carry out operations, they mobilise part-timers, 'amateurs' or freelance activists, often with respectable day jobs and with no police record of involvement in extremist violence. Whereas the typical international terrorist group of the 1970s and 1980s was linked directly or indirectly to a state sponsor, the typical 'new' terrorist groupings are able to operate autonomously, finding their own private sources of funding, expertise, weapons and explosives. This higher degree of autonomy, their sophisticated use of new global communications systems, and their tendency to switch their activities rapidly from country to country, make them a far more difficult quarry for the intelligence and police agencies engaged in combating international terrorism. Perhaps most worrying of all the features of the 'new' international terrorism are set out below.

First, the groups involved appear willing to engage in the mass murder of civilians without any qualms, regarding this as a necessary part of striking a blow at their hated 'enemy'.

Second, because the 'new' terrorist groups are driven primarily by religious fanaticism they can find a ready pool of young zealots prepared to martyr themselves in the course of terrorist attacks, and it is especially difficult in open democratic societies to protect the public against the suicide bomber, as the recent experience of Israel tragically demonstrates.

Third, and most troubling of all, the 'new' terrorists' propensity for indiscriminate mass terror causing massive casualties combined with their sophisticated interest in new forms of terrorist tactics and weaponry has, in the view of a number of leading experts, considerably increased the probability that 'new' international terrorists will acquire and use weapons of mass destruction.[2] The threshold of weapons of mass destruction use by terrorists has already been crossed by Aum Shinrikyo, a fanatical Japanese religious cult, which used Sarin nerve gas in attacks on Matsumoto in 1994 and in the Tokyo subway system in 1995.[3] The Tokyo attack caused 12 deaths and more than 5,000 injured, but would have been infinitely more lethal if the terrorists had disseminated the nerve gas in a more concentrated form. The Aum Shinrikyo cult was organized internationally as well as in Japan, and had many of the features of the 'new' terrorist groups, including the use of activists with respectable day-time jobs and those with no police record whatsoever. The cult had also been investigating the possibility of using nuclear and biological weapons. Sadly, it is highly unlikely that the cult is the only 'new' terrorist group that has made serious efforts to obtain weapons of mass destruction.

In assessing the threat posed by the 'new' international terrorism it is important to pay close attention to the activities of Ramzi Yousef, for in almost every respect he is its true archetype. Yousef is serving life imprisonment in the US for his role in masterminding the 1993 World Trade Center bombing in New York and for plotting to blow up a dozen US airliners over the Pacific region within the space of 48 hours, the so-called 'Bojinga' plan. He has used numerous aliases and false passports in travelling the world in his terrorist activities, and investigators had great difficulty in establishing his true identity. According to an interview he gave to *Al-Hayat*, he was born in Kuwait, his father came from Pakistan, and his mother is a Palestinian. He claims to be a Palestinian 'by choice', makes no secret of his hatred for the United States for its policy of support for Israel, and admits to being part of a Liberation Army of militant Muslims in many countries waging a campaign to punish and undermine the US.

In almost every respect Ramzi Yousef appears to be the very model of the 'new' terrorist. No conclusive proof has been found to link him to a specific state sponsor of terrorism. He has been truly transnational in his activities, having been based at various periods in Afghanistan, the United States, Pakistan and the Philippines, and having acquired his impressive expertise in bomb-making during his period as a student of computer-assisted electronic engineering at a college formerly known as the West Glamorgan Institute of Higher Education in Swansea in the United Kingdom.

Nor is there any doubting his willingness to inflict massive casualties in his terrorist conspiracies. Following his arrest, the FBI have told agents that his real plan in the World Trade Center bombing was to topple one of the Center's twin towers on to the other one, thereby killing perhaps as many as 250,000 people, and that he had considered releasing a cloud of cyanide gas in the huge explosion, and was only deterred from this by the expense involved. If Yousef's 'Bojinga' plot to blow up 12 US airliners had not been thwarted by the lucky discovery of a computer file in Yousef's apartment in Manila outlining the conspiracy, it would have killed at least 4,000 passengers and crew. He did not flinch at huge civilian casualties, and, if his statements to the FBI investigators are to be believed, he had no qualms about using a chemical weapon against a crowded urban target.

The additional factor which made Yousef's 'new' brand of international terrorism so lethal was his skills and knowledge as a master bomb-maker. In the eyes of experienced observers his expertise in this field was quite exceptional. An example of this was the miniature bombs he planned to use to destroy a dozen US airliners. Liquid nitro-glycerine, hidden in contact-lens solution bottles and hence easily hidden from Airport Security checks, was linked to a Casio wristwatch timer and detonators that had been hidden in shoes. Yousef tried out his device on a Philippine Airlines flight from Manila to Tokyo in December 1994. He used the aircraft toilet to assemble his bomb while the plane was *en route* from Manila to Cebu. He then placed the device under his seat and left the aircraft at Cebu. Several hours later it exploded, killing a Japanese man and injuring a dozen other passengers. It is as miracle that the pilot was able to land the aircraft safely following the explosion.

One continuing puzzle about Ramzi Yousef is how he was able to fund his extensive international travels and terrorist activities. If we discount the possibility that he was helped by a state sponsor of terrorism, then the most likely explanation is that he was financed by the wealthy Saudi dissident, Usama bin Laden, blamed by the US government for masterminding the bomb attacks on US embassies in Nairobi and Dar es Salaam in August 1998 in which 263 people died. When Yousef was arrested in Pakistan, he was staying in a guest house set up by bin Laden for Afghan war veterans, and was in possession of bin Laden's address. Moreover, the Abu Sayyaf terrorist group in the Philippines, in which Yousef played a key role for a time, obtains much of its funding from bin Laden's brother-in-law. Whatever the truth about Yousef's possible connections with bin Laden, it is difficult to disagree with the conclusion of the US Department of Defence's *Strategic Assessment* (1997):

> He [Yousef] may be the prototype of a new type of terrorist being produced in large numbers by the Middle East: young, full of religious and ideological zeal, technically skilled to a high degree, and determined not only to kill Americans overseas but also to bring terrorism to the American heartland.

Why Civil Aviation is Still a Popular Terrorist Target

It is clear from Ariel Merari's opening essay in this volume that although there has been a welcome decline in the total numbers of incidents of international terrorism, including aviation terrorism, since the late 1980s, civil aviation remains an attractive target for international terrorists, and attacks on civil aviation targets of all kinds, including airports and airline offices, constitute approximately 10 per cent of all international terrorist incidents annually.

What are the basic reasons for this? Brian Jenkins, in his article on Aircraft Sabotage, reminds us of some of these. He refers to the:

> ... terrorist tendency to target public transportation, which offers terrorists concentrations of people – mostly strangers – in enclosed environments, and generally poses little security challenge and allows easy escape ... commercial aviation historically has been a favourite target of terrorists who have viewed airliners as nationally-labelled containers of hostages in the case of hijackings, or victims in the case of sabotage .

We should also bear in mind that terrorist attacks on civil aviation have often proved extremely effective in yielding valuable tactical objectives, such as massive world-wide publicity, the release of terrorists from prison and the payment of large cash ransoms.

Moreover it would be a grave error to assume that changes in the nature of international terrorism have rendered attacks on civil aviation obsolete. On the contrary, the 'new' terrorism, and the extreme Islamic fundamentalist groups which present the most dangerous international terrorist threat as we approach the end of the century, have already clearly demonstrated their fascination with civil aviation as a potential target. This is evidenced, for example, by Ramzi Yousef's bombing of a Philippine Airlines plane, and his 'Bojinga' plan to blow up a dozen US carriers in the Pacific region. In December 1994, the extreme Islamic fundamentalist group, the Algerian GIA (Armed Islamic Group) hijacked an Air France Airbus in Algiers and killed three passengers before flying to Marseilles. They threatened to fly the plane on to Paris and blow it up in mid-air over the city, but on 26 December, France's GIGN (National Gendarmerie Action Group) stormed the plane, killed the hijackers, and rescued 170 passengers and crew. And in May 1996 Israeli police disclosed that a Hezbollah agent had succeeded in smuggling nearly a kilogram of RDX plastic explosives on a Swissair flight from Zurich and through Ben Gurion airport in Israel. It is believed that he was planning to blow up an EL AL plane leaving Israel. The police stated that a Sony clock radio was modified to disguise the bomb and the device would have been detonated by the use of a hollow rubber tube which replaced the AM antenna. It has similarities to the device used to blow up Pan Am 103. The presence of the terrorist and the conspiracy to bomb an Israeli airliner were only brought to light when the terrorist was severely injured in an accidental explosion in a Jerusalem hotel on 12 April.

In the wake of the carnage caused by the bombings of the US embassies in Nairobi and Dar es Salaam in August 1998, in which more than 260 people died, and the US retaliatory cruise missile strike against Usama bin Laden's base and training camps in Afghanistan, it is clear that there is an intensified international terrorist threat against the US and its allies. Bin Laden and the fanatical Islamist terrorist network he sponsors have threatened further attacks. The US embassies were clearly targeted because they were seen as clear symbols of their hated enemy, the Great Satan, and because they were viewed as soft targets.

Other US soft targets, such as US businesses, tourists, airliners, check-in-desks, as well as potential targets within US territory, therefore need to be in a higher state of vigilance in the light of the increased threat.

To sum up, the threat of international terrorist attack against civil aviation is not only very real, it has recently been considerably heightened. Statistics on the annual totals of terrorist incidents may therefore be dangerously misleading and must not be allowed to create complacency. While we are likely to see fewer attacks than in the past, and while the improved aviation security measures in certain countries have certainly deterred and prevented many attacks, it is clear that the major international terrorist players have the resources, sophistication and ruthlessness to find the weaknesses in global aviation security and to commit mass murder on the airways on a scale we have not seen before. One of the key lessons we should have learnt from the Air India, Lockerbie and UTA bombings is that *qualitative* changes in terrorists' *modus operandi* can lead to a massive increase in the lethality of attacks: Lockerbie alone accounted for no less than 40 per cent of all victims of international terrorism in 1988.

Terrorist Use of WMD, and Other Emerging Threats

Marvin Schaffer has discussed in depth in his article in this volume the growing missile threat to civil aviation, and Bruce Hoffman has provided a judicious assessment of the potential threat to air cargo integrators. It would be remiss, however. in this concluding article, to overlook other emerging dangers posed by terrorists developing new methods to attack civil aviation.

One important area of innovation is in the choice of explosives. In recent years, terrorists have favoured the use of powerful military explosives such as PETN, RDX and TNT, easily obtainable by means of theft, purchase, or supply by a state sponsor. But as the explosive detection technology now being deployed to counter the terrorists is focused almost exclusively on military explosives, so the terrorists have a strong incentive to try switching to explosives or pyrotechnics which do not conform to the classic formulas for military explosives. For example, peroxides can be used as stand-alone explosives or as oxidisers in composite explosives, triacetone triperoxide (TATP) can be synthesised from acetone, as is believed to have been used in a number of terrorist incidents. Moreover, the methods for making this and a wide-range of nitrogen-free explosives, are easily accessible in do-it-yourself explosives manuals. Aviation security managers and personnel need to be fully aware of the growing interest being shown by terrorist groups in a wide range of non-detectable home explosives, and explosives detection technologies capable of identifying non-nitrogenous explosives need to be developed, tested, and if found effective and commercially viable, deployed generally in the world-wide aviation security systems. In addition to using nitrogen-free explosives terrorists could make use of a wide variety of incendiary devices, self-igniting materials, hydrides and phosphorus.

Details of the above and many types of 'exotic' explosives can be easily obtained from bomb-making manuals and from the Internet. The materials needed to manufacture home-made bombs of this kind are easily obtained. It is clearly common sense for aviation security authorities to develop contingency plans and crisis management capabilities to deal with terrorist attacks using weapons of this kind against airport terminals, check-in-areas, and airline offices, as well as airliners in flight and on the ground. Nor should it be assumed that 'new' terrorist groups are unaware of the possibilities of non-nitrogenous explosives; for example Hamas has used TATP in its bombing campaign against Israel.

The traditional weapons of the terrorist, such as conventional explosives and incendiary attacks, continue to appeal to terrorist groups for three major reasons: they are easy and cheap to obtain, they have a proven capacity to cause considerable loss of life, serious injury and destruction of property, and they are relatively safe and simple for the terrorists to use. Nevertheless, since the Sarin nerve gas attack carried out by Aum Shinrikyo against the Tokyo subway train system on 20 March 1995, there has been a heightened concern that other terrorists might also resort to the use of chemical, biological or nuclear weapons. It has been established that the Aum Shinrikyo cult had shown great interest in acquiring a nuclear weapon capability, and had experimented with anthrax, one of the deadliest and most accessible biological weapons. A few grams of pulmonary anthrax are sufficient to kill 99 per cent of the victims who become infected.

Many scenarios on the possible use of the weapons of mass destruction by terrorists envisage whole cities or regions being targeted, but the Aum Shinrikyo Sarin attack on the Tokyo subway train system is a tragic reminder that improvised relatively crude chemical, biological or nuclear weapons can be used with deadly effect against more specific targets. In considering the emerging threats to civil aviation we need to bear in mind that airport terminals and airliners offer prestige targets for this type of attack.

To counter this type of threat the national security authorities need to ensure that they have a strategy for dealing with the threat. Although the threat is of relatively low probability it is so high-consequence in its potential lethality and destructiveness that it is vital to ensure that counter-terrorism intelligence agencies have the capability to obtain early-warning of emerging weapons of mass destruction threats and to rapidly acquire accurate information about the NBC weapons programmes of states involved in sponsoring or supporting terrorist groups or perhaps using their own agents to engage in covert terrorist attack. It is obviously also extremely important that all states in possession of fissile materials take the necessary measures to prevent such materials falling into the hands of terrorists. (It is worrying fact that in the former Soviet Union the security controls over nuclear weapons and materials and the associated technological expertise have been so lax that some leakage to terrorist groups and states has most probably already occurred.)

A major consideration for contingency planning by aviation security authorities should be to prepare for the possibility of NBC attacks against civil aviation targets. This must involve close co-ordination with all the relevant agencies including the emergency services and the public health authorities, in order to ensure the early detection of biological and chemical weapon attacks and the deployment of effective medical treatment reduce casualties. The experience of Japanese authorities in the Tokyo subway attack underlined the importance of ensuring that the emergency services have specialist knowledge, training and equipment available to deal with a chemical or biological attack, including medical teams trained to deal with the effects of chemical poisoning and biological toxins. In many countries, the main focus of this expertise has been within the defence forces: as in the Tokyo case, the civilian authorities need to be able to deploy such units with great rapidity to meet such emergencies.

There has been a growing debate in the literature on another widely perceived emerging threat; the possible use of information warfare or cyber-warfare by terrorists aiming to cause temporary disruptions to or sabotage of vital computer networks. The term 'cyber-terrorism' has been widely used, but it may be inappropriate if what we are dealing with here is sabotage *per se*. If the terrorists' aim is to create a wider climate of extreme fear and to exploit it for political purposes, then this is a clear case of cyber-warfare being used as a terrorist tool. One can undoubtedly identify potential targets for terrorist cyber-war in the civil aviation industry; for example the air traffic control systems on which the whole industry depends. It so happens that the current level of computer technology used in some of the largest aviation countries ' air traffic control centres is rather poor. Ironically this makes them rather less vulnerable to disruption by cyber-warriors. However, as the US, Britain, and other big aviation countries modernise their computer networks, the air traffic control systems will become far more vulnerable. It is a future threat the industry cannot afford to ignore.

However, taking full account of these emerging threats, including from weapons of mass destruction, it is clear that by far the most serious current emerging threat at time of writing is the one described by Marvin Schaffer in an earlier article: it is the threat of missile attacks against civilian airliners. To date, almost all such attacks have been against military aircraft. If terrorists were to succeed in shooting down several jumbo jets by means of missile attack it would have a disastrous effect on public confidence in air travel, and hence inevitably on the well-being of the industry.

Weaknesses in Aviation Security

However, even if one discounts the emerging threats (for which very few aviation countries have any serious contingency plans), the global civil aviation system is still riddled with loopholes. Ten years after Lockerbie most countries have failed to introduce regulations to require the screening of all hold baggage on international flights. And most countries are still unwilling or unable to ensure positive baggage reconciliation to prevent any unauthorised unaccompanied bag from being placed being placed on board an aircraft. The civil aviation industry itself estimates that 8,000 bags are misrouted on the world's airways every day. Only a tiny proportion of the world's airports are equipped with the latest enhanced X-ray machines, which are capable of detecting plastic explosives of the type used to bomb Pan Am 103. The sad fact is that despite all the statements of good intent to improve aviation security another Lockerbie could happen today. Indeed we know of at least three cases of planes being blown up in mid-air since Lockerbie, with the loss of all on board, and one near miss when the bomb exploded killing a passenger and injuring 10 others.[4] However, the Philippine Airways plane was able to land successfully.

Nor should it be assumed that the US, by far the world's largest aviation power, is ahead of the rest of the world, in reaching high security standards. As Brian Jenkins' article on US aviation security, published in this volume, makes clear, the US lags behind both the UK and continental Europe in many respects.

The 1990 President's Commission on Aviation Security, set up after Lockerbie, recommended action to ensure that effective explosive detection systems were developed and installed in US airports, and to ensure positive baggage reconciliation – the twin pillars of security against sabotage bombing. Unfortunately, these recommendations were never properly implemented. For years, the US government and the industry chiefs have quarrelled over who should foot the bill for security improvements and about which security measures and technologies should be used.

Following the crash of TWA 800 off New York in July 1996 with the loss of all on board, President Clinton set up the White House Commission on Aviation Safety and Security under the chairmanship of Vice-President Al Gore. President Clinton pledged that security to and from the US would now cover 'every plane, every cabin, every cargo, every time'. But when it became clear that the FBI could find no evidence of a bomb, the Gore Commission's emphasis began to switch to air safety issues. As Brian Jenkins makes clear in his article on US aviation security policy in this volume, the Commission made many excellent proposals for improving aviation security. Unfortunately, however, the Commission's findings were not mandatory. The aviation industry has consistently opposed the proposal for positive passenger-baggage reconciliation on the grounds of cost and because of their fear that it would disrupt their service. As a weak compromise measure, the Federal Aviation Administration recommended that either a baggage reconciliation or screening for explosives would only be required for passengers identified as requiring stricter security checks. In their Initial Report, dated 9 September 1996, the Gore Commission recommended that:

... the government purchase significant numbers of computed

tomography detection systems, upgraded X-rays, and other innovative systems.[5]

In response to this the Federal Aviation Administration ordered 54 advanced explosives detection systems, a very small number when one considers the sheer size of the US civil aviation system. Moreover, it is estimated that the total programme for upgrading US aviation security could take up to five years.

One might have expected that the US would emerge as the clear world leader in aviation security policy and practice. After all, the US is the world's leading aviation power, with more than 7 million aircraft departures per year from US airports, and more than 17 per cent of all international scheduled passengers flying on US carriers. The US pioneered airport boarding gate security measures against hijacking, and has spent more than any other country on research into explosives detection technology. Pan Am 103 was targeted because it was a US airliner, and the overwhelming majority of passengers were Americans. Yet the standards of security in their domestic aviation are extremely low: practices such as curbside baggage check-in and electronic ticketing and the use of low-paid and poorly trained security personnel produce greater vulnerability.

As Omar Malik's article on British aviation security makes clear, the UK has made great improvements in this field since Lockerbie. Despite its shortcomings, the overall level of airport security compares very favourably with that achieved in the US. The UK has a comprehensive statutory framework for aviation security, a regulatory agency with strong powers to monitor and enforce the implementation of aviation security regulations, and requirements for positive baggage reconciliation on all flights, the screening of hold luggage on all international flights for explosives, and the screening and reconciliation of all transfer baggage.

However, the picture in the rest of Europe is very mixed, with many countries screening as little as 5–10 per cent of hold baggage for explosives. It would be irresponsible to identify countries and airports with particularly glaring security weaknesses. Sophisticated terrorist groups search for weak links in security and we should not be making their task any easier. However, a widely reported example of lax aviation security occurred at Orly Airport in Paris in September 1998, when a police officer was able to smuggle a large fake bomb hidden inside a personal stereo in his hand luggage through security checks and an X-ray machine and into the departure lounge.[6] Moreover, although French anti-terrorism measures require one in four of all bags to be searched, the private companies responsible for the security checks are so seriously undermanned that they have been unable to carry out their tasks effectively.

This is by no means the first time that weaknesses in French aviation security have come to light. In August 1995 a French labour union member representing flight crews on France's Air Inter airline complained that security screening of luggage on France's domestic flights was inadequate. The labour union stated that for several months it had been pressing the Ministry of Transport to require 'systematic surveillance' of checked baggage on flights within France. It is worth bearing in mind that in the previous December, Algerian terrorists had hijacked a French Airbus to Marseilles, and in 1995 there were bombings in Paris by Algerian extremists. The labour union affirmed:

> It is scandalous that domestic flights can be classified as non-sensitive (and) it is easy to imagine the disastrous consequences of an explosion on board an airliner or a hijacking.[7]

The above examples should help to dispel any complacency about the state of aviation security in the wealthy major aviation states. All have weaknesses which need to be rectified, because national aviation security measures must be the building blocks of an enhanced global response, and because any country in the world may become the recipient or the target of a hijacking, or the target of a sabotage bombing of an airliner or an attack on an airport.

However, if we are surveying the global aviation scene for weak links in the chain of aviation security, there is no doubt that we find the gravest weaknesses in the airports of Africa, South Asia, the CIS states, and parts of Latin America. Many of the countries are so poor that they cannot afford to acquire up-to-date modern security equipment or properly trained and effective security personnel. In November 1996, the International Federation of Airline Pilots' Association warned that airports in most African countries had no security screening and were unable to provide airport perimeter security or access control to sensitive areas of the airport.

Towards Enhanced Global Aviation Security?

In his interesting discussion of the politics of aviation terrorism, Peter St John concludes by proposing that as the underlying political causes of much aviation terrorism are rooted in conflicts spilling over from the Middle East, the best way to eradicate the problem of air terrorism would be to resolve the basic conflicts in that troubled region. The conflicts he has particularly in mind are the Israeli-Palestinian conflict and the conflicts between radical Islamic fundamentalists and their opponents. It is certainly highly significant that since the initiation of the Israeli-Palestinian peace process and the Oslo accords, international terrorist attacks undertaken in the name of the Palestinian cause have declined dramatically. Despite the current impasse in the Peace Process it is already clear that the Palestinians have gained more by politics and diplomacy than they did from twenty-five years of terrorist activity.

However, the conflict resolution approach to eradicating aviation terrorism or international terrorism in general is far from being a panacea. Some terrorist groups do not have political demands or aims which could even be the subject of negotiation and compromise with governments and the international community. Should governments be willing to make political agreement with those responsible for the Luxor massacre, for example, or for the carnage of the bombing at the US embassy in Nairobi, or for the Lockerbie and UTA bombings? Should the Japanese government have negotiated with the Aum Shinrikyo cult? Obviously not. Much of international terrorism, including aviation terrorism, is committed by 'irreconcilables', fanatics motivated primarily by hatred and a belief in their right to commit mass murder to avenge alleged injustices and to destroy their enemies in a kind of holy war. Peter St John infers that the international community should be seeking means of conflict resolution to appease the Islamic fundamentalist terrorist groups, but the reality is that these groups have been responsible for some of the worst of the recent terrorist outrages and any attempt to compromise with them would conflict with the values of democracy, human rights and the rule of law, and would inevitably encourage more terrorism. The only morally and politically defensible response to these *hostis humani generis* is to mobilize the international community in a global effort to outlaw them, to combat them, and to capture those guilty of atrocities and bring them to justice.

International judicial co-operation to bring terrorists to justice must therefore play a vital role in any global strategy for enhancing aviation terrorism. There have been some notable successes in the 1990s in bringing leading terrorists and former terrorists, such as Carlos the Jackal and Ramzi Yousef, to trial and securing convictions. But the huge inherent difficulties that arise in efforts to obtain their rendition for trial are all too clearly demonstrated in the case of the two Libyan Lockerbie suspects indicted in the US and Scotland in 1991. As this volume goes to press it is by no means certain that the Libyan regime will co-operate in allowing them to be tried in the Netherlands under Scots law, as offered by the British and American governments.

As national aviation security systems are the essential building blocks of an effective global response to aviation terrorism, a first priority must be for the richer aviation countries to help their poorer neighbours to take effective practical measures to overcome the vulnerabilities of their airport and airline security by helping to get their standards up to scratch. To overcome this problem, the G7 governments should join forces with the aerospace and civil aviation industries and, with the help of a modest passenger security levy, set up an international aviation security fund which would provide soft loans, grant-in-aid, and subsidised airport security equipment to those countries that cannot afford it. In addition there is a need for a more ambitious and well-resourced international programme to train the aviation security managers and staff of low income countries in all the techniques and skills needed to combat the ever-changing terrorist threat. Some G7 states, such as the USA, Canada and Britain, already provide some bilateral training and technical assistance, but it is a drop in the ocean compared to what is needed. The ICAO Mechanism for financial, technical and material assistance to the USA with regard to aviation security, using a strategy of assessment and follow-up, has been of enormous help to States seeking to upgrade their capabilities.

However, as Dr Assad Kotaite, President of the Council of ICAO, observed in a speech in Washington in January, 1997:

> Enhancement of the aviation security posture globally has some way to go before we can claim success. States must be encouraged to formulate and apply the political will which regulators and industry can rely on. The success of the human factor and technical elements of a State's aviation security

> endeavours is predicated on the existence of such political will. There is no alternative.[8]

In the course of the same speech, Dr Kotaite called for the full and complete implementation of the Tokyo, Hague, Montreal, and Supplementary Protocols to Montreal, Conventions. He went on to urge that:

> we must also examine ways and means of enhancing the enforceability of ICAO Annexes. ... An answer might well be found in the introduction of international technical inspections, or in other words safety/security system audits, which call on States to rectify disclosed deficiencies. ICAO, as an international body, should be empowered to closely check the implementation of safety and security standards and carry out regular inspections.[9]

As one who has long argued for an international aviation security inspectorate, under the auspices of ICAO, I was greatly encouraged by Dr Kotaite's clear perception of the potential advantages of such an initiative.[10] By coupling the important safety issues with security, he made the case still more compelling. I would wish to go even further and establish the means of enforcement of the ICAO minimum standards. Any country that persistently failed to bring its security into line with ICAO standards could be made subject to sanctions by the international aviation community.

Yet, however desirable this approach may be as a means of enhancing global aviation security I see little prospect of it being adopted. The establishment of a more powerful global aviation security regime would require a degree of consensus among the member states of ICAO, and many states would strongly resist any attempt to limit their sovereignty in aviation security matters. For the foreseeable future we will have to make do with improving national aviation security standards and bilateral and regional co-operation. In our new world disorder, governments, regulatory agencies and the aviation industry are more likely to try to muddle through, responding to each crisis as it comes. Disjointed incrementalism rather than coherent global regime building is the order of the day.

NOTES

1. For a clear and cogent account of the 'new' international terrorist trends, see Bruce Hoffman, *Inside Terrorism* (London: Gollancz, 1998).
2. See for example, the US Department of Defense study. *Terror 2000: The Future Face of Terrorism*, Washington, D.C. Department of Defence, May 1994) and Richard A. Falkenrath, Robert D. Newman, and Bradley A. Thayer, *America's Achilles Heel: Nuclear, Biological and Chemical Terrorism and Covert Attack* (Cambridge, MA: The MIT Press, 1998).
3. For a useful discussion of the Aum Shinrikyo case see James K. Campbell, *Weapons of Mass Destruction Terrorism* (Seminole, Florida: Interpact press, 1998), pp.51–71.
4. For statistics on cases of sabotage bombing of aircraft see the article in this volume by Ariel Merari, pp.13–22.
5. The Final Report of the White House Commission on Aviation Safety and Security, 29 June 1997, 3.15, p.23.
6. See Susan Bell, 'Airport's flawed security exposed by police "bomb"', *The Times*, 5 Sept. 1998.
7. Quoted in Pinkerton: Risk Assessment Services, 12/34, 25 August 1995.
8. Text of Address by the President of the Council of ICAO, Dr Assad Kotaite, to the International Conference on Aviation Safety and Security in the 21st Century, Washington DC, 13–15 Jan. 1997, p.3.
9. Ibid., p.4.
10. See Paul Wilkinson, *The Lessons of Lockerbie* (London: RISCT, 1989), pp.20–21.

Bibliography

Captain Thomas M. Ashwood, *Terror in the Skies*, New York, Stein and Day, 1987.

'Aviation Security: How to Safeguard International Air Transport': Conference at the Peace Palace, The Hague, January 1987.

Peter Clyne, *An Anatomy of Skyjacking*, London, Abelard-Schuman, 1973.

Steven Emerson and Brian Duffy, *The Fall of PanAm 103*, London Futura, 1990.

Alona Evans, 'Aircraft Hijacking: Its Cause and Cure', *American Journal of International Law* 63 (1969), pp.695–710.

Alona Evans, 'Aerial Hijacking'; in M. Cherif Bassiouni (ed.), *International Terrorism and Political Crimes*, Springfield, IL, Charles C. Thomas, 1974.

Alona Evans and John Murphy, *Legal Aspects of International Terrorism*, Lexington, D.C. Heath & Co, 1978.

Thomas B. Hunter, 'The proliferation of Man-portable SAMs', *Counterterrorism and Security Report* 6/2 (July/August 1997), pp.2–5.

Brian M. Jenkins (ed), *Terrorism and Beyond: An International Conference on Terrorism and Low Level Conflict*, Santa Monica, CA, Rand, 1982.
Brian M. Jenkins, *The Terrorist Threat to Commercial Aviation*, Santa Monica, CA, Rand, 1989.

Salim Jiwa, *The Death of Air India Flight 182*, London, W.H. Allen, 1986.

Edward McWhinney, *Aerial Piracy and International Law*, New York, Oceana, 1973.

Edward McWhinney, *The Illegal Diversion of Aircraft and International Law*, Leiden, A.W. Sizthoff, 1975.

Ariel Merari, 'International Terrorism and Civil Aviation', *Inter* 1987. Jaffee Center for Strategic Studies, Jerusalem, 1987, pp.71–84.

John F. Murphy, *Punishing International Terrorists, The Legal Framework for Policy Initiatives*, Totowa, NJ, Rowman and Allenheld, 1985.

David Phillips, *Skyjack*, London, Harrap, 1973.

Report of the President's Commission on Aviation Security and Terrorism, Washington DC, 1990.

Report of the White House Commission of Aviation Safety and Security, Washington DC, 1997.

Peter St John, *Air Piracy, Airport Security and International Terrorism*, New York, Quorum Books, 1991.

Rodney Wallis, *Combating Air Terrorism*, Washington DC, Brassey's (S), 199.

Paul Wilkinson, *Terrorism and the Liberal State*, Basingstoke, Macmillan, 1986.

Paul Wilkinson, *Lessons of Lockerbie*, London, RISCT (Conflict Studies 226), 1989.

Paul Wilkinson, 'Designing an effective international aviation security system', in *Airports and Automation*, London, Thomas Telford Services Limited, 1982, pp.17–26.
Paul Wilkinson, 'Aviation Security: The Fight Against Terrorism', *Interdisciplinary Science Reviews*, 1999, Vol.18. No.2, 1993, pp.163–73.

Paul Wilkinson (ed.), *Technology and Terrorism*, London, Frank Cass, 1993.

Abstracts of Articles

Attacks On Civil Aviation: Trends And Lessons
ARIEL MERARI

Although the first attempted aerial hijacking occurred in 1931, attacks on commercial aviation became a major problem only in the late 1960's. The beginning of the phenomenon can be accurately pinpointed in time: In 1966 there were only five attacks on commercial aviation and six attacks occurred in 1967. In 1968 there were already twenty-nine attacks and in 1969–94 attacks. The attributes of these attacks are discussed below. Government authorities and airline companies had to adjust rapidly to a new reality and to find ways to cope with a new threat. This article also examines the adequacy of their response.

The Politics of Aviation Terrorism
PETER ST. JOHN

During a 30-year period, the hijacking of civil aircraft has been aimed at Western governments, not only to disrupt, but to bring about political change in the Middle East. Using Pan Am 103 as a case study, this article examines the confusion in US decision-making, which attempts simultaneously to conduct a rational foreign policy and confront international terrorism in the Middle East. The Pan Am 103 episode also demonstrates the conflicting agendas and enormous lack of co-operation between US government agencies. Finally, it is suggested that solving the root problems of the Palestinians and improving American relations with Iran may go a long way toward eradicating the scourge of hijack terrorism.

Aircraft Sabotage
BRIAN M. JENKINS

Commercial aviation historically has been a favourite target of terrorists who have viewed airlines as nationally-labelled containers of hostages in the case of hijackings, or victims in the case of sabotage. The terrorist assault on airliners set off a deadly contest between bomb makers and airline security which has continued for the past quarter century with security gradually gaining. In the early 1970's, more than 30 percent of international terrorist attacks were targeted against commercial aviation; it is less than 10 percent today. The 1970's saw at least 18 attempts to sabotage aircraft with eight crashes. The 1980's saw an increase in attempts with six crashes. There have been far fewer attempts in the 1990's with only one crash.

Aviation Security and Terrorism: An Analysis of the Potential Threat to Air Cargo Integrators
BRUCE HOFFMAN

This article utilises empirical rather than anecdotal evidence to examine, based on the historical record: the nature of the terrorist threat to commercial aviation; the patterns of international terrorist activity within the context of the threat posed to aviation; and, the motives of terrorists who target commercial aviation. Based on the above analysis, it concludes with an assessment of the terrorist threat to air cargo integrators specifically.

The Missile Threat to Civil Aviation
MARVIN B. SCHAFFER

Near the end of 1997, more than a year after the event, the circumstances of the TWA 800 crash are still uncertain. Could it have been caused by a man-portable missile fired by a terrorist? There is no evidence in the recovered wreckage thus far to support that theory and investigators are leaning toward other answers. Although the author has no basis for questioning their finding, it is useful to review some related facts concerning man-portable anti-aircraft missiles, including both history and technology, and attempt to dispel a few myths. Could such an event occur in the future? The answer is yes.

The Role of International Aviation Organizations in Enhancing Security
RODNEY WALLIS

This article describes the role of the international organisations, ICAO, IATA, ECAC and the ACI, in enhancing civil aviation security. It offers a brief explanation of their different roles and shows how they link to provide a worldwide security structure for the benefit of the air traveller. Their strengths and weaknesses are considered and their different approaches to aviation security implementation discussed. The commercial organisations' mandate to provide *safe, regular and economical* air transport is reviewed and a practical example of security enhancement is given. The sterile lounge concept, experienced by all air travellers using British airports, is used to demonstrate the link between facilitation (making things easier) and security.

Aviation Security Before and After Lockerbie
OMAR MALIK

The destruction of Pan Am 103 in British airspace re-energised British aviation security activity. Creditable efforts were made by both the British government and the British civil aviation industry. There were advances in political direction, administrative system, security standards and in security consciousness. The security of British aircraft overseas is dependent upon other states meeting their responsibilities. HMG has not taken a holistic view of aviation security. Government unwillingness to contribute to the industry's costs underlies its failure to develop a constructive partnership with industry. Nonetheless Great Britain can reasonably claim to have led the world in the pursuit of higher aviation security standards.

Aviation Security In The United States
BRIAN M. JENKINS

The crash of TWA Flight 800 off the coast of New York on July 17, 1996 prompted an ambitious program to upgrade aviation security in America. The initial circumstances of the crash suggested that the plane had been brought down by a terrorist bomb or, some suggested, a missile. Nearly a year after the event investigators concluded that mechanical failure was the more likely cause of the crash. Flight 800 apart, many observers felt at the time that substantial improvements were long overdue if only to bring American security in line with that in Europe. New security measures were recommended by a White House Commission that, when fully implemented, will lead to the most significant increase in aviation security since the adoption of full passenger screening in the early 1970s.

Enhancing Global Aviation Security
PAUL WILKINSON

The author concludes that because of a combination of factors in the international strategic environment, terrorism will remain an intractable problem well into the next century, and civil aviation will remain an attractive target. He reviews some emerging threats not dealt with in the earlier articles in the volume. Techniques of conflict resolution and 'peace processes', though valuable in certain contexts, are not a panacea for ending terrorism. Existing weaknesses in aviation security should be rectified and measures taken to counter emerging threats. The need for strengthened international judicial co-operation, and for an effective global regime for the inspection and enforcement of high airport security standards is stressed. The author is not optimistic that these goals will be achieved, although some national aviation authorities are making significant improvements.

Notes on Contributors

Bruce Hoffman is Reader in International Relations and Director of the Centre for the Study of Terrorism and Political Violence at the University of St Andrews, editor of the journal *Studies in Conflict and Terrorism*, and author of *Inside Terrorism* (1998).

Brian M. Jenkins formerly headed RAND's terrorism research programme before moving to Kroll Associates. He was a member of the Gore Commission on Aviation Safety and Security and is now a consultant for RAND, Santa Monica.

Omar Malik is a former British Airways Captain and chairman of the British Airline Pilots' Association's security committee. He gained his PhD at St Andrews University for a thesis on British aviation security policy. He is now a contributor to the International Security Programme at the Royal Institute of International Affairs, Chatham House.

Ariel Merari is Professor of Psychology at Tel Aviv University and one of Israel's leading academic experts in the field of terrorism studies. He is Director of the Research Unit on Political Violence at Tel Aviv University, and has made a special study of aviation terrorism.

Peter St. John is Professor of Political Studies at the University of Manitoba, where he has specialized in intelligence studies and Middle East politics. He is author of *Air Piracy, Airport Security and International Terrorism* (1991).

Marvin B. Schaffer is a senior consultant for the RAND Corporation, Santa Monica.

Jim Swire lost his daughter, Flora, in the Lockerbie bombing. For ten years he has been the spokesman of the UK Families Flight 103 group. He is a medical practitioner.

Rodney Wallis is a former Director of Security of the International Air Transport Association (IATA) and helped draft the third, fourth and fifth editions of Annex 17 (Security) to the Chicago Convention. He is author of *Combating Air Terrorism* (1993).

Paul Wilkinson is Professor of International Relations and chairman of the Centre for the Study of Terrorism and Political Violence at the University of St Andrews.

Index